MIRAGE AND TRUTH

THE MACMILLAN COMPANY
NEW YORK · BOSTON · CHICAGO · DALLAS
ATLANTA · SAN FRANCISCO

MIRAGE AND TRUTH

by

M. C. D'ARCY, S.J.

NEW YORK

THE MACMILLAN COMPANY

1935

Imprimi Potest
        JOSEPHUS BOLLAND: PRAEP: PROV: ANGLIAE

Nihil Obstat
        ARTHUR J. SCANLAN, S. T. D.
                                Censor Librorum

Imprimatur
        ✠ PATRICK CARDINAL HAYES
                                Archbishop, New York

New York, May 9th, 1935

PRINTED IN THE UNITED STATES OF AMERICA
BY THE POLYGRAPHIC COMPANY OF AMERICA, N.Y.

INTRODUCTION

WE are living in an age which is conspicuous for propaganda, and in writing this I am not thinking of the Press and of the advertisements which deface our streets. I mean political and social and, if the Oxford Group Movement be accepted as a witness, religious propaganda. The wish to communicate and share a cause is almost proportionate to the belief in it, and, therefore, there is nothing surprising in reformers and revolutionaries writing tracts; but it is a new portent when the liberal arts are converted into forms of propaganda. The Communists have persuaded the artist that he must not stand idle in the market-place, and as a result a large number of writers are given over either to supporting a current social ideal or else fashioning one of their own. I have set out, therefore, in this book to portray the religious and Christian ideal in contrast with some of those which have recently been put forward, and I have chosen as subjects for comparison not religious rivals nor a dominant social ideal such as that of Communism. The latter would require a treatise in itself, and the former should yield, I think, to the prior question of the superiority of religious, and specifically Christian belief over any other ideal. I have preferred for these reasons to take one or two writings which exhibit the spirit and longings of some of the nobler individuals of our time, and after having discussed their merits to challenge them and any other view whatsoever with the glory that belongs to the Christian faith.

The task to be undertaken is not easy. The Christian conception of life is both high and far-stretching. To do it full justice the intricate wisdom of its philosophy, the sayings and writings of its saints and mystics should be called upon. To write popularly of it is almost to desecrate it, while to treat it seriously is to court failure. Aquinas retired in despair before he had completed his *Summa* and Augustine achieved success only by humbling himself in personal *Confessions*. The trouble is that the greatest of subjects cannot be appreciated, much less mastered, with a relaxed mind and tossed off like a glass of wine ; and yet it must be presented to those who have neither time nor talent for long study. One might answer, and answer truly, that good will and patience can prepare the appetite for God's mysteries, and this answer would absolve theologians from much writing could they be sure that such virtues were ever present. As it is, all I can hope is to avoid too facile argument and too recondite a language. It needs a John the Baptist to prepare a way which will be plain, and I think it would be an insult both to the glorious theme glanced at in the following pages and to the reader to try to persuade him that truth can be won at an easy price.

In writing this I do not forget the conviction of St. Paul, expressed in the letter to the Romans, that the evidence for God's existence is plain, and that those who deny it are heavily to blame. We must remember, however, that the persons whom St. Paul has in mind are those " who detain the truth " and so hoodwink the simple, and that if we ask ourselves who are now the teachers and the wise and who are the simple, the answer is very difficult. The coming of education to almost all seems to put them in a different position from those in St. Paul's time who were dependent in so much on others for their beliefs. But if they are more learned they are not for that necessarily more wise, for what they read has no formative influence. It is rather a hotchpotch of views which may too easily reduce the minds of the mass of people to a sticky, flaccid mess. Moreover, the learned themselves are overweighted by the more than Babylonian load of philosophy and science. Sciences have accumulated with startling rapidity these last two hundred years and in each science theories have multiplied like spermatozoa and died, but not before the report of the theory spread and disturbed and flustered the minds of students. And at the back of science lay the shadow of philosophies which scouted the possibility of acquiring truth outside the world of sense. The modern generation, therefore, starts with a prejudice, whether it be learned or barely educated, and it is not responsible for this start. That this is no exaggeration a little experience will show, and we have only to ask our neighbour his convictions, to wander off to any lecture given indoors or out of doors or to pick up the journals which are devoted to philosophy and science, to find confirmation of it. It has been my good fortune to have the opportunity of often listening in Hyde Park at the Marble Arch to the speakers there and to hear the arguments among the crowds. It is disheartening to hear the assumptions which are made in most cases. There are a number whose methods show a discipline in a materialistic system, and poor as their arguments are they carry much weight because they are " slick " and clear; it is the work of a professional against an amateur. But what is more alarming is that those who are listening are pleased with their assumptions, have no regard for the old or the traditional, and thrust aside any appeal to absolute standards, to the belief in a God or in immortality. Similarly, in discussion circles at the Universities and in cities it is rare to hear an argument which dares to go beyond the experience of the senses and science. The professional thinker is strangely tolerant of all sorts of views which to some of us seem just exasperatingly nonsensical, such as that all our thought is a kind of physical behaviour, that there is no difference between dreaming and awakening, that the room I am sitting in is as much part of me as my body. These and many other similar strange tenets are tossed about in lecture and senior common

8

rooms, so often, in fact, that there is a real danger for one who takes up philosophy of spending most of his days learning the technical words of a new theory in order to be able to refute it, though it was never worth a long refutation. The truth is that even in the circles of austere philosophers the human element enters in as much as it does in Dr. Coulton's monasteries. Whereas the expert is tolerant of some fashion and prepared to take seriously the proposition that he is no more than the table he is looking at, he is unduly annoyed, if it be suggested that the word soul is in place in a discussion on psychology, that the science of ethics has a number of loose ends unless some kind of immortality be admitted, that a serious philosophy cannot avoid the conception of a divine being. He seems to feel that the game is not being played fairly, that he is being forced to be present at some séance. Not long ago the head of an Indian University paid a visit to a celebrated English University. He asked if he might meet some of the philosophical faculty in it, and one of its members told me afterwards as a good story that his purpose had been to ask them their views about God. Being troubled by the moral and spiritual condition of his students he wished for advice on the teaching of theology. The question had proved very embarrassing. Those present shuffled their feet and would say nothing and were inwardly amused by the childishness of the question. No doubt as Mr. Ackerley has so delightfully described in his *Hindoo Holiday* an

Englishman can be disconcerted by a Maharajah asking him at a first meeting his private views on God, but the matter goes deeper than that. The fact is that theology has become a detached pavilion or annex to the house of philosophy, with the result that by neglect it has become covered with cobwebs and some do not even know of its existence. A tendency, too, which I can only call most unfortunate has developed in certain quarters of taking religion as something apart, an experience, as it is called, which is variously estimated according as one has enjoyed it or not. What is to be said of this will be found in the sequel.

This being the position, it is not surprising if a number of people when asked confess that they know nothing about God, that their lives and their thoughts go on without Him and they have been taking for granted that what used to be believed about Him in past ages is no longer true.

What then I propose to do is to set the theistic and Christian ideal in competition with those that have taken its place and have found favour. To judge from the remarks made in essays and books the attempt will be greeted with derision or surprise by many. For my own part it is to me a matter of continual surprise that human and intelligent beings should be so hostile to the Christian ideal. To turn away with a sigh from a vision of supreme happiness which offers a joyous end to man's sorrowing journey is intelligible if that vision be no more than a fancy or a dream. To hate it, that indeed is strange. Cordelia was misjudged by her father—I should like to be able to show that the ideals so much admired now are but Goneril's and Regan's; " Wisdom and goodness to the vile seem vile : Filths savour but themselves. What have you done ? Tigers, not Daughters, what have you performed ? The soul like the King is not on the heath, and there is no longer much comfort in the air ! "

LEAR. O, cry you mercy, Sir.—
　　　　Noble Philosopher, your company.
Edgar. Tom's a-cold.
GLOUCESTER. In, fellow, there, into the hovel; keep thee warm.

CONTENTS

MIRAGE AND TRUTH

MIRAGE AND TRUTH

CHAPTER I

COMPETING IDEALS

TALKING to the most learned audience of his
time, St. Paul told them that he was able to
give them true tidings of the God whom they
ignorantly worshipped, the God who was not far from
them, for in Him they lived and moved and were.
These words may sound arrogant, if quoted now by
the Christian, but they are well worth reflection, for
they may imply that we have been on the wrong track
in our thought about God. That the world has always
been haunted by the sense of some divine being can,
I think, be made out from history. Even the atheist has
felt it his duty to conduct a campaign against what he
denounces as an illusion, and the fever of his rage does
not seem to be fully accounted for by the evils for
which religion has been said to be accountable. The
rage is too personal for that; there is a note of rebellion in it and we do not rebel against nonsense, even
pernicious nonsense; we look behind to a culprit and
an author and we are not content till we have slapped

his face and shown that we at least are not taken in by
his devilry and do not intend to submit to it any longer.
So it is that the divine illusion takes shape and becomes
a living being in the very derision of the idea. Or to
put this in another way. When we have no expectations we are not disappointed, and the more savage the
disappointment the higher must have been the ideal
which has been frustrated. Now does not this suggest
that the militant atheist is the victim of a high hope,
that he has pitched his dream as he thinks too high and
the God of his inner longing has not corresponded with
the images of it which he has met and been told of in
his human journeying? And so with that strange madness which takes hold of men he has slain the thing he
loves and driven his knife into his own heart. When
that genius Nietzsche wrote of his annihilation of God,
he does not cry out with glee ; he whispers in anguish,
" We have slain God," and his misery is a measure of
his triumph.

If such be the case, we have found a new sense in
the words, " whom you ignorantly worship." There
is the story of the man who, going to see the king whom
he reverenced, mistook the chamberlain for him and,
disgusted with the vulgarity of the man, decided to have
no more to do with kings. There is also the story of
Joan of Arc who went straight into the presence of the
Dauphin and bent her knee to him though he had been
disguised. The first is unfortunately coming to be the
more common experience. So many now do not find

in the versions of theology or religion with which they are acquainted a view of God or life which is tolerable to them, or—and this brings the blame to our own door —their desires and thoughts are so darkened that they cannot recognize truth and what is to their good. For one or other of these two reasons they are " ignorant." I am not referring to those who would quit themselves of their responsibilities by pointing a finger of scorn at the conflicting creeds—" how those Christians love one another ! "—nor to those even who avail themselves of the claptrap about a religion of love and the folly of the Churches. Half a minute's reflection is enough to make clear the silliness of such talk. A religion of love has never meant anything by itself ; if it is more than a vague sentiment it is bound to take shape in terms of doctrine and rules of action, to bring within its scope reverence and fear and justice and wisdom and bring a solution to the manifold problems of human nature. And as for the divisions within Christianity and conflicting creeds, is it not human to err, and if error can be embraced must not truth have its rivals ? Suppose for a moment that there was any value in the objection, then it would be sufficient for another to claim my name and character for me to lose all right to them in the public esteem. How convenient a way this would be for getting rid of objectionable views and objectionable persons, a way far more swift and decisive than the method of the English Government to oust recusant families of their rights in penal days !

No, the difficulty does not lie there, but in dealing with a generation which has heard stupidity parading in the garment of religion and has not had the opportunity or occasion to distinguish between the counterfeit and the true. Even the Bible has in this matter proved a cause of unbelief. If ever evidence were needed for the wisdom of the Catholic Church in keeping the reading of the Bible under some control, it could be found to-day. In open-air controversies almost invariably the unbeliever takes as his weapon of attack the account of God as given in the Old Testament. It is a rock of offence to the modern mind, and if the Bible is to be taken fundamentally and literally, we have indeed in it pictures of God which are just an invitation to unbelief. This has been obvious to the Church of orthodoxy and tradition, and so it has always claimed to be the interpreter of the Bible, and it is able to show that within its scheme of life, in the perspective of Catholic teaching, the Old Testament stories are in truth a manifestation of the way of God with man and man's correspondence with the divine will. But this is scarcely known at all to the majority of men and women to-day. Not only are they left defenceless by a mere reading of the Old Testament, but everywhere around them they are hearing of prehistoric discoveries, of men who were never fully men; they are told that the old conceptions of cause and effect are outworn, that we know either too little or too much about nature to use it as evidence for God, and at any rate its circuit has been widened so infinitely that the shipshape universe and well-ordered kingdom of the Sovereign Lord with his sceptre have passed away as many another childish belief. They think that they can see for themselves that a reverent agnosticism is far finer than a dogmatism which is inclined to put fetters on free thought, and that finally science advances and theology gives way step by step. This is the inheritance of many of fine intelligence and generous disposition, who would be glad to believe.

In face of this unbelief which can grow faster than any weed in a garden, the believer feels himself at times almost impotent. He has so much to cut down and the slashes of his knife seem to have so little effect, and he finds to his cost that it is so much more difficult to fight an attitude than a person. Not only are the majority of men more moved by emotion than reason, so that the sharp rattle of the syllogism leaves them unmoved and faintly antagonistic, but their emotion is only the outworks of an attitude which cannot be grasped because it is round and slippery and lies behind the mind of its possessor. Mr. Chesterton in his novel, *The Ball and the Cross*, depicted two sane men, the Atheist and the Royalist Catholic Highlander, fighting round the world and always being interrupted by some insane theorist. This fight has been called in more pedantic language the logic of extremes, and it would be well if in the combat of believers and unbelievers both parties would take the trouble to think out to its furthest limits the theory of life they hold. If this experiment be tried it will be found that there is hardly any room for the agnostic. The atheist says there is no God, and I suppose generally goes on to say that we can get on better without Him. I will invite the atheist later to explain how this can be. For the moment let us consider the agnostic. He, so I understand, refuses to follow the atheist; he says in effect that God may exist but he cannot be sure of it. Now such an attitude is a most difficult one to justify, though, so far as one can guess, a very large number of people adopt it. It implies that God has not given sufficient evidence of Himself to warrant us acknowledging Him. I do not know whether this will strike the reader as very curious. If it does not then let him stop to reflect what he means by God. Not surely some indifferent being, not a drowsy creature whose presence can be as neglected as that of the White King in *Alice in Wonderland*, and yet this ought to be the conclusion of the agnostic. In his version the Lord God who made Heaven and earth, upon whom all depends, " in whom we live and move and are ", the God who is the source and end of all things, our doom and our bliss, this God is to have left Himself without a witness ! It is as if one were to say, " There may be a blazing fire in this room, I really cannot say," or " I may for all I know have had a parent, but really I am not in the position to judge." Agnosticism, therefore, is atheism without its logic; to say that God may be is to say that He is not, for God could not be a vague hypothesis, could not play truant in His own creation or shift His responsibility. When Jehovah said, "I am who am," He meant to declare His sovereign being, and there could be no intelligent creature who could think away that sovereignty.

This criticism of agnosticism does not however touch those who for a period are sorely troubled in spirit because they cannot honestly convince themselves that God exists. Such does seem to be a passing state of many, and they have to act in conscience according to the certainty or uncertainty of their belief. But it is a different thing to say that agnosticism is a sensible philosophy, in fact, the true philosophy, and to be worried at one's own inability to be convinced. In the latter case it is a personal problem ; in the former it professes to be a proposition of universal application, and as such it is a self-contradictory assertion. I might add that even those who have it as a personal problem should ask themselves whether the difficulty does not contain in its very expression the answer one way or the other.

The agnostic may however take up what has here been written and urge that I have misconceived his position. He does not deny that there is a God. All he says is that God cannot be known, and it is conceivable that God should have left man to work out his own salvation in dependence on himself. It is true that this is a slightly different form from the one already criticized, and it contains a belief which is common with that of the theist. God is essentially mysterious to us, and the history of mankind shows quite clearly that the thoughts of men have been far from clear as to the divine nature. Every sort of attribute has been predicated of Him, and many of the best thinkers have copied Job and putting their hand before their mouth have exclaimed that His ways are not as our ways and His thoughts not as our thoughts. If this were all that agnosticism meant, then there would be small room for protest. More however is evidently in the minds of those who say this. The conclusion of their argument is that the inability to know all about God absolves them from paying God any attention at all. They postulate a complete ignorance whereas the theist admits only a degree of ignorance, and there is all the difference in the world between these two attitudes. Quite apart from the fact that so many of the greatest minds throughout history have longed to know more about God and have sought diligently to do so, and also that religion of itself shows this ineradicable tendency of men to have intercourse with Him, it is certain, as I shall try to argue later, that the mind can ascertain something about the divine nature, and to deny it this prerogative is to do both God and human nature wrong. If the knowledge has been small in content and thin of texture, it is nevertheless something, as the agnostic himself seems to admit in his very discussion about the notion of a divine being, and it is a preparation for that more complete knowledge which, as the Christian holds, has been given to us by divine revelation.

Agnosticism, therefore, is a tempting position to take up, but it is a half-hearted one. We like to keep God in the rear as a reserve to call upon in case of necessity, and to keep awkward questions in the background, and there are some who feel their pride and liberty are touched if they commit themselves too quickly to an old truth. Such claims to independence of judgment are, alas! too frequently a surrender to human respect and a herd instinct. To strike an attitude before the multitude, whether present actually in the body or before the mind's fancy, tickles the feeble in soul. But even when a state of suspended judgment seems to be a dictate of wisdom it would be well to think out resolutely all the consequences of choice—and so compare the alternatives before us. By so doing we may be unpleasantly surprised, but at least we shall have the comfort of knowing that we are not putting blind eyes to telescopes, burying our heads in the sand and doing what all the psychoanalysts tell us is so bad for our mental health, namely, living in a world of makebelieve.

Before assisting the reader to do this let me remark on another odd form of conduct which those who have suffered often assume. It has been already mentioned and consists in blaming God for misfortune and then denying Him. Let us suppose that a man has been a believer and that he has been happy. Then comes some intense disappointment. It is natural for man to seek to throw the blame for this on someone, and it is perhaps equally natural in the first moments of anger to

23

be tempted to accuse God. But what is easy to understand in a fit of anger becomes strange and unintelligible
as a fixed determination. And it becomes still more
unintelligible when the sufferer passes from blaming
God to cutting Him out of his life and out of existence.
It does not follow because God has been in part responsible, let us say, for the hurt that He cannot exist. The
opposite seems to be a more logical conclusion, for if
God did do one harm He must be there, and one does
not usually blame a man for knocking one down when
he does not happen to have done so and in fact does
not exist. But the situation is even more odd than this,
for the determination to rebel and the permanent mood
of rebellion are surely an unconscious witness to the
continued existence of God. Men do not rebel against
a figment ; they are merely glad or sorry to have found
out its true nature, whereas here there is a morose or
savage or bitter feeling of satisfaction in the thought
that they are able to show to someone their independence and their wrath. But even this is not the end,
for what they are really doing is to cut off their nose
to spite their face. How common is this conduct !
The schoolboy who deliberately does badly in an examination out of a sense of injury, the man who refuses to
enjoy his holiday because of a quarrel, the lover who
loses his love, giving her up because he is jealous.
Similarly, with those who turn their backs on the God
they used to believe in ; they are but hurting themselves. If we ask ourselves candidly the question, which

is the preferable picture and alternative, to be alone with suffering in a world whose purposes, if it have any, we do not know or to be in communion with One who is able to make out of suffering a joy, who knows our condition and can be more to us than a father or mother or lover, one too who has good intent with regard to us which stretches into illimitable time, can there be more than one answer? To choose the first is to rob ourselves and others too of the one hope which makes life endurable. Just because we suffer we say, "It can't be true and I won't have it true," and instead of getting true joy out of our choice we exile ourselves fatally from any chance of reaching a promised land.

This brings us to the alternatives of atheism and theism. In the last paragraph I may already appear to have loaded the dice heavily against the former. It is not true, the atheist may say, that I am robbed of great expectations. Those who abandon religion and the worship of a God are freed from a superstition, and, if you consult them, they will tell you that they experience a great sense of relief. An intolerable burden has been taken from their shoulders. There is no denying that religion has often been an oppression of the spirit, that fear is inextricably bound up with it and that it stands in the way of a genuine self-determination. All of us, it is true, have met men and women who have finished with religion and God, who, according to their own account, have broken the net and are free. But I do not think that such evidence proves very much.

Certainly some conceptions of God and some forms of religion have been baleful. The late Sir Edmund Gosse in his *Father and Son* has described for us a nightmare religion typical of the perversions the worship of God may undergo. But all that this comes to is that evil may be done in the name of the best, and when this happens the evil is of the most atrocious kind according to the adage, *corruptio optimi pessima*. We do not blame education because it has been abominably mis-used at times, nor government because it has been tyrannical. It should be obvious that the means taken as regards any of the great issues of life are capable of distortion, and the greater the issue the more serious the danger. A great issue is not simple. There are not many ways of milking a cow or shearing sheep, and it is only by accident that a number of the activities of man, his virtues and vices are brought to bear on these operations. But when the M.C.C. have to take decisions, the London County Council to decide about Waterloo Bridge or slum areas, the League of Nations to consider the peace of the world in Eastern affairs, we are in the presence of issues which cannot be settled by a man jumping up and saying, " Let us play the game and all love one another." So many of the activities of man are involved, so careful a balance has to be preserved, that it needs the genius to arrive at a right solution. Society has been built up and pre-served by the development and harmony of a mass of instincts, tendencies and forces. Appeal has to be made to the various qualities in every individual. No leader would have a chance of success if he ignored altogether personal ambitions, if he refused to allow any kind of reward for public service save the consciousness of having done well, if he resolved never to use the weapon of fear, to exercise only the virtue of mercy, to have no reserves, to treat all alike. As we know only too well, there are very different estimates of human nature, different systems of education and government according to country, time and type of person. This is not to make truth relative, but to adapt it to the power of the recipient, and so hard is this that the grossest mistakes may be made. That religion which is con-cerned with all that is of the highest in human nature, having to watch most carefully the disposition of the worshipper, the violence of the passions, which has to train, shape and elevate man to do what his lower nature abhors, to mould what is rough till it becomes a vessel of most delicate and precious worth, should have blundered is even less surprising than that medicine, the art of healing, should have done much mischief to the body in the course of its development. The moral is to choose a good doctor, not to do without any doctor at all.

For a fair comparison we should take the best that theism can represent. Now whether we argue from examples or from theory, the superiority of theism stands out markedly. The atheist seeks to deny this when the argument is from examples by pointing to excellent men and women who have had no belief in God. Before deciding this appeal a distinction should be made. Men and women differ very much not only in natural endowments of body and mind, but also of character. Some are of happy disposition and yet selfish, others melancholy but quick to appreciate the feelings and condition of others. There is no sharp line which can be drawn between natural and acquired virtue. Nevertheless, the distinction remains, so that we can at least say that it is much easier for some to be benevolent and self-sacrificing than it is for others, in the same way as we know that some are ill-tempered and shy while others are easy-going and sociable. Now I do not deny that the virtue of the good unbeliever is personal and acquired; what does not seem so evident is that it has been acquired with the same splendour of personal effort, the same heroism as has clearly animated the believer. When one is summing up the unbeliever a certain amount has to be left over to natural enthusiasm brought to a head by a cause. The cause is there also with the Christian, but it is one which demands infinite holiness in the individual as well as devotion. Theism will not allow a blind man to lead the blind into the ditch; it casts out all who would come to the feast without a wedding-garment. It is indeed terrible in its insistence on the inner purity of those who would seek communion with God. It matters little that the natural character be weak; the Curé d'Ars was a timid, under-sized man; that it be obstinate and proud; the young Gonzaga was as obstinate as a mule; that it has been coarsened by the depravity of a Charles de Foucaulx. No matter, for the character is like wax in the hands of their spirit and the grace of God. What strikes everyone who is an unbiased critic is the power of self-control in the saints and the stretch of their virtues. They reveal to other men what man can be; they smash the body to atoms and come forth a living flame with a body newly refreshed; they unearth the hidden beauty in human beings who have been passed over as the waste product of humanity and they thread together on one golden cord of the love of God virtues whose existence was scarcely known, whose combination seemed incredible, ardour and patience, meekness and power, detachment and affection, lowly hope and high humility. But, above all, the saints possess some secret of peace, as if, like the successful lover, they were in possession of their heart's desire and in this fulfilment some joy sang within them to which all their faculties made response. They are not lonely nor stoical, they are well acquainted with sorrow and they embrace pain, but everywhere they go they are accompanied by the sunshine of spring.

This we know to be the ideal of the Christian life, and the knowledge comes not from some theory of what ought to be but from the evidence of so many who have embodied this ideal. Now when confronted with the various advertisements and prospectuses of the best life which can be led on this earth, it is the end and not the beginning, the successes and not the failures which ought to decide for us our choice. Consequently the argument of those who have given up religion should receive little attention, unless they can claim with truth that they have tried and tested it to the full. If we appeal to those who have gone the full distance and not fallen out with a broken wind we shall find invariably that they have experienced an incomparable joy and enjoyed a fullness of being which can only be called divine. Here then is their evidence, and their behaviour bears out their evidence and leaves an imperishable memory with mankind. Have the other advertisements anything to rival this? Certainly not the many invitations to a new liberty which serves only as a cloak for indulgence, nor again the decent life of mingled activity and repose, the sheltered scholar's life, the busy or adventurous days, the take what comes and go ahead view. Aristotle and many another have sketched the portrait of the happy life. They cannot be said to have kindled the imagination of man. Plato comes nearer to what we want, but he is out of court as he was a firm believer in the gods. Indeed, some of the best alternatives to the one I have given are doubtful evidence. Plotinus has stirred many, as he still stirs the minds of thoughtful men like the Dean of St. Paul's. I do not think however that the atheist will appeal to him, as he uses the language of the theist and is in mind and heart much more in sympathy with the believer than the atheist. Curiously the same holds true of Spinoza. He was treated as a rebel by the Synagogue, and he writes for the most part as one who knows no personal God, but as he draws near to his ideal the language changes and his inspiration grows more and more like to that of the great worshippers of every age.

Now I know that some when they hear this will murmur and call to mind friends of theirs, apparent unbelievers for whom they have the greatest admiration, and they will compare them with others who are professing Christians, who are pious and nevertheless singularly unattractive. What to say to this? Quite honestly the difficulty is not easy to dissipate, though for a reason which does not weaken in any way the view so far maintained. When we are arguing about human nature we have to keep to general rules and to collective experience. When we apply these rules to the individual we have always to be on our guard, for there are at least two dark places in the history of each particular man. We do not know exactly the influence of heredity and environment and the effect of causes physical and mental on the momentary or chronic mood he is experiencing, and secondly we only know from outside what is going on in his consciousness and habits of mind. This is one reason why the Christian is forbidden to judge others. Not that we are thereby rendered incapable of coming to sound conclusions about human beings; we have an idea of what the ideal and perfection of human nature should be and we can tell when men and women fall short of it; but of the extent of blame and merit which any particular individual deserves we have no exact knowledge. As a consequence it is very difficult to discuss the virtue of this man or that, and if I seem to have done it in quoting the nobility of certain saints, that is because they are but illustrations of a type of life which is followed by an innumerable number. As on their own evidence they are representative of a definite creed and a definite manner of life knowingly and willingly chosen, and this way of life has similar effects on many others who also choose it, it is not unfair to make them an argument for the perfection of that ideal. When, however, we turn to those who have given up a belief and yet practise virtues which are undeniable, we are not in the presence of representatives but of exceptions. Moreover, these exceptions in so far as they are conspicuous for any virtue reach forward to the Christian ideal, so that it would not be unfair to argue that their excellence is a tribute to theism. I will not press this, however, because unless it be developed with extreme care it might seem to rely on a false assumption or to be arguing in a circle; and the argument put forward here can be so stated as to be independent of any such development. For the same reason we can leave aside the problem why some who are sincere theists and practising Christians remain so unattractive. A few remarks on this will not however be wasted. The principle of all growth in intelligence and personality which is to be found therefore in a special manner in

the Christian life is unselfishness ; and by this I mean
first that to be wise we must yield whole-heartedly to
the teaching of truth without prejudice and selfish
regard. From the beginning the child comes to a
knowledge of itself by interest in other things and
persons, and if in education the mind of the young
should be active, there is demanded also a certain
passivity in order that that mind should be rightly
informed. All of us, too, are well aware that our best
work is done when we are occupied wholly with the
objects which we are studying or making and that here
self-consciousness is an embarrassment and may be a
curse. What is true of the mind holds also for the
character. The man who puts himself always first is
a long way from perfection ; he has not even begun
to climb the heights and realize within himself what
true love and heroism mean. This principle is indeed
the infallible test and sword of division in the struggle
of a man's soul, and it helps to explain the riddle of the
Christian's failure. Even the best can by a slight twist
serve selfish ambitions and desires ; God is not loved
for Himself, faith becomes an advantage and not a
grace, prayer a comfort and not a sacrifice, constant
attention to religious practices and duty the act of a
Pharisee ; and all this is fatally easy and comes to pass
without the man being fully aware at any moment of
the twist which he is giving to all that should exalt
him. " If you but knew the gift of God," but the gift
like some priceless necklace has been taken to pieces

and melted down. This desecration is the result of the all-pervasive tendency to self; and no fault consequently can be found with the ideal.

So much, in passing, for this problem. Nothing further need be said about it because what we wish to know is whether unbelief can offer an alternative worthy of consideration. The case for atheism has been put by Bertrand Russell, but his words are so well known and their inconsistency so often pointed out that I prefer to quote a view which is at least hopeful. This has been described in a way which many have found attractive by Charles Morgan in his book, *The Fountain*. He says :

Pressing upon him was the thought that, though the contemplative life was rare, the contemplative desire was universal, being, in the spirit, what the sexual desire is in the flesh, the prime mover of mankind. Contemplative stillness, he said, is but the name for a state of invulnerability, and to be invulnerable is what all men desire. Even the desire for immortality, springing from fear of death and having its fruit in the doctrine of the resurrection, is less than the desire to be invulnerable, being part of it. . . . To enter by some means into a condition that excludes all but itself is every man's purpose, he wanted to create within him a retiring place which the fret of common existence and the hot breezes of desire and fear and ambition should be powerless to disturb.

And again :

. . . to establish a citadel within the sensible world without first annihilating the senses, to build the spirit not with the deaths of mind and body but with their selective and disciplined vitality, to lead the whole man, fearless and undivided, into that peace which is invulnerable and requires no immortal armour—these were his

purposes and he knew that to achieve them a man must be stronger
than the Christian saints. Not only must he be wedded in spirit
to nothing mortal and conquer that fear for the loss of earthly
pleasures which the saints also overcame, but he must be without
terror, as they seldom were, of the impact of earthly forces and,
as they could never be, of the loss of immortality.

The aim of the hero in these passages is to attain to
a degree of invulnerability and that without any surrender
of the use of the body and joy of the senses. The
questions therefore to be asked are whether such a state
is attainable and whether if attained it would be that of
ideal perfection. The author of the book seems to
leave the first question undecided, as he obviously takes
the ideal seriously and never in word abandons it; on
the other hand, his hero certainly does not achieve his
desires, and the one who draws closest to the ideal is
the German who is dying and so wounded as to be an
invalid deprived of the proper glory of his body. I do
not believe that such inconclusiveness is accidental; it
is inevitable. Invulnerability is the ideal, but if this
means a revised version of the old Stoic philosophy,
then it can be bought only at the price of cutting out
of one's life all that would disturb it, of fasting from
sensuous joys and sorrows which come from interest
in and sympathy with others. The soul must steel itself
against disappointment of hopes and deny itself expectations and joys which may be taken away; it must retire
behind a wall which hides from view the spectacle of
a beloved Hector dragged at the chariot wheels of a
triumphant enemy. And if this be what is meant it

inculcates an asceticism more severe than that of any Christian and for a motive which every Christian would scorn. Better to declare openly for an enlightened selfishness than to rush to a fastness to feast on nothing but the shadow of one's heroism.

But this can scarcely be meant. The invulnerability must belong to an ideal state, be like a well of stillness in which the sounds of an immortal beauty are heard. There will then be the joy of complete self-possession and the presence of some beloved visitant. But who is this visitant? In the theory, so far as I can see, it is nothing but experience enjoyed in quiet and the cult of it brought to a fine art. Let us leave aside the question whether there be not something anæmic in this or at least factitious, something which makes us think of gold-fish in the darkened atmosphere of an aquarium and sigh for hurly-burly virtues. The real trouble is that no matter how much we practise such an art we shall never be invulnerable. The world we meet in experience is not one for soft gestures and dreamy incantations, it is full of apparent contradictions; it opens out vistas of beauty and hides all in pitiless rain; there are gleams of hope and lampblack ugliness; we respond to its enticements and are torn by its thorns. Even its highest experiences can be but intermittent and the symbol of its love is a bleeding heart. By a process which has been studied in the East and has had its adepts also in the West a spirit of deep reverie can be induced which passes in its prolonged stages into what

I may call a simulacrum of peace. But there is a great danger in such so-called mysticism, as the mind drops down the hood of its eye and withdraws into a state of passivity. There is rest here for a while from outward disturbance, but the rest comes through a diminution of energy, from a conjuring away of reality, and the mind is not so much taken up into a new strength and love by the contemplation of some surpassing object as hazed by an illusion of nothingness. This lotus land is no stage on the way to beatitude; it is not even a respite for all who are invited to journey there. To some this way lies madness; to others after-affects, which, like those of sleeping sickness, do permanent injury to the moral character.

But even supposing that such states of passivity were a precious boon they must always be the possession of the few, and it is a universal ideal for which we are seeking, one which all should have hope of reaching, both wand-bearers and bacchants. There is many a citizen of New York, many a worker in the shops of Manchester, many a seaman and stoker who would rapidly call the bluff of anyone who talked to them of invulnerability, and there are those on whom a responsibility has been thrust by nature or accident, mothers, guardians, officials of all kinds, who have to be constantly sensitive to dangers present and to come. In considering ideals we have always to bear in mind " the dumb, suffering people; reviled and outcast, yet pure and splendid and faithful "; all conditions of life and estate, the cripples as well as the strong, those who die in the prime of their youth as well as those who drag on into a neglected old age. The author of a remarkable but too little known book called *The Prison*, H. B. Brewster, realized this. He too was looking for an ideal, an ideal which has some resemblance to that of *The Fountain*. But the Prisoner in the book gives more thought to it and he is aware too of the many difficulties he must meet. It is this fastidious and sincere handling of the subject which makes the solution he arrives at so nearly right. As it stands there are fatal gaps due, I think, to a lack of full understanding of the all-inclusiveness of Catholic theology. The Prisoner tries at first to make the best of his lot by withdrawing into the haven of his own mind.

Ah, if hours such as the one I am now writing in could but last the livelong day! If there were no gnawing desire, no dark annihilation—only this lucid peace! I will tame these hours and teach them to come when I whistle for them, as other prisoners tame spiders or mice.

But he soon finds out that he cannot so tame his moods and cast out pain and all the other intrusive devils.

Surely it was a stranger that spoke in my name the words of a dreamer and a stoic. Behold the worm exclaiming to the heel that crushes it: " I thank thee, for thou art the symbol of my thoughts. I have called thee on my own head; thou art the minister of my will."

Then in his meditations comes the suggestion of an

ideal which is put forward by so many as an alternative to theism and, one might add, to despair. This consists in the immortality of our works. " It is a modern view too ; we are supposed to live for our fellow-creatures and for our posterity as our ancestors lived for us. . . . Many things grow ; empires grow, science grows, even wealth can grow ; all is not ephemeral." But this too he dismisses as unsatisfactory. " It is the evangel of the happy few whose works are masterpieces, but it will not apply to our dealings with those around us nor to the bulk of the legacy of centuries." If we leave behind us good we also bequeath much evil and mystery, our mistakes, our follies, a long trail of mischief. It is all very well to signal out the great artists and thinkers.

But we, the millions who have no talent, who raise no structure, perhaps not even so modest a one as an accumulation of money or of learning—it were a derision for us to boast that we last, merely because the play of cause and effect is eternal. It is not enough to tell me that my action will go on bearing fruit for ever, and that therefore nothing is insignificant. Unless some firm tie so connect the hours of my life that they all belong as different phases to one same growth, or as different scenes to a well-knit drama, what matters it that to-day perish at midnight or that its traces be ineffaceable? I say that if all my strivings are not gathered into an imperishable sheaf, these successive and aimless efforts, these impulses, these moods whereof I live from hand to mouth, do not gain a whit of dignity or significance for all the dust they may raise. Clouds of dust are but clouds of dust, however far they may blow.

This criticism is final and fatal to all views which take away the substance from our personality to find it again in some artistic immortality, some temple of delight to which the builders have no entrance. Between the lines, too, of this criticism we can read also the dissatisfaction with any ideal which does not give meaning to the apparent mystery of man's life. Strangely enough Brewster in his own solution falls under the very condemnation he has pronounced. The story of the development of his case in the diary is too subtle and exquisite to be shortened, but the main plan is as follows. Like Proust he is bewitched by the princely power of memory and what goes on within the soul. There in memory is the healing power of thought and an interior language. "Who speaks these words? . . . We go on listening when we awake to something within us which is as the tuning of instruments, and until they have all found their right pitch we have no will to work." Here is a presence which binds together the past hours and the present, the most intimate and sure revelation of the self, or rather not the self since it is above the self and in others as well as in the Me. And in this phase the Prisoner feels that this core must be also the core of everything ; otherwise all others and all beings are cut off and unreal.

I am cut off from all contact unless I am the image of God. I am cut off from the universe if the universe is not the image of me. I stretch out my hungry arms and they enfold but shadows, if in what they clasp there is no answer to this great cry of love in which I recognize myself, and in which I melt away. What furious and divine selfishness is this, that asserts and sacrifices itself at the same moment ; that refuses to hear of aught but itself and resolves itself into allhood !

I should like to go on quoting from this narrative, but it must suffice to say that he does not rest here, for he still seems to be subject to illusion. He is doubtful whether as the subject of his everyday thoughts he is more than a sentient memory, whether his self is anything more than the meeting-place of these memories, and as for his thoughts, how does he know that they are more than the pageantry of a dream ?   One answer comes to him.   The universe around cannot be an unsubstantial pageant, for

there is a voucher behind the very things I touch which imparts to them their apparently intrinsic evidence, and without which they would crumble into a meaningless heap of disconnected perceptions. But must there not also be a warrant for this broader reality which vouches for the immediate one ; and again a warrant behind that warrant? If men can agree at all, must there not ultimately be a grand warrant the same in all and the framework of each of them? What if it be this that they call God. Then properly speaking he is the condition of all reality, and as there is nothing by reference to which we can perceive him as real in the same manner as we perceive other things by ultimate reference to him, his existence must both escape the tests which apply to all other forms of existence and yet be the object of the highest certitude.

Here the Prisoner draws very close to the theist solution, and part of his difficulty, namely, the doubt about external reality, would be felt less by modern philosophers who are rabidly realist. The solution is accepted neither by him nor by the listeners to the diary. We

have no guarantee, it is argued, that the succeeding
layers of thought and the succession therefore of vouchers
correspond with the real order of the universe. At
most we can suppose that this structure so conceived,
if it be a universal experience, is a form of thought by
the assistance of which we can open fields of culture
otherwise inaccessible. And even this is unsatisfactory,
as the sceptic amongst the listeners argues. The multitude of men and women in the world do not live by
these high and abstract thoughts. They are one-sided,
and a religion made up of them is always helped out by
quite other considerations. " Their religion agrees
with them because of the small heed they take of it."
But they cannot live entirely on religion ; " this mainspring does not work one-tenth of the wheels." The
ideal embodied in it no more covers all that a man
should be and do than a top-hat clothes his body.
And so the diary of the Prisoner shows him once more
puzzled and dissatisfied. It is too awful a thought that
the full story of the countless millions of men should
be that " they have lived in darkness, that there has
been no escape for them from the cage of personal
vanities and interests, no outlook, no background, no
beauty, no joy, and that they have rotted in communion-
less selfishness ". And yet the idea he has been express-
ing,

this inner life with its joys of companionship in a cherished ideal,
its sense of the presence of God within us, its pride in a secretly
tended flame destined gradually to illuminate the surrounding

darkness seems . . . the futile effort to collect into one hour of consciousness the infinite and conflicting aspects of reality.

But out of this last despair comes the solution which is the culmination of Brewster's thought. To understand it we must remember that he has been working forward from his inward experience vouchsafed to him by memory. He distinguishes between various kinds of memory. There is one which is purely mechanical, " a colourless, indifferent residue of sensation," which works " as a clerk might keep an account of his pen-and-ink expenses regardless of the contents of his writings." When the residues have accumulated into a mass " important enough to be the cause of a sensation that contrasts with the ever-varying flashes that pass before it, the polity has acquired a permanent self." But this is not what we usually mean by the self and by memory. It is the qualitative memories with their different contents and combinations which makes us think of ourselves in terms of our reputation or our work or friends.

We live in a web of associated memories ; our general map— the chart thanks to which we know more or less clearly where to put what, recognize analogies, make order out of chaos and accumulate experience—is a network of memories. And one of ourselves, the loudest-voiced one, the one we usually think of when we say I, corresponds to the spot on that map where the most frequent and familiar memories cross each other, as the railroads of a country at its capital.

Now if there were to occur a sudden distribution of forces and if the activity in this network were concentrated in one tract giving it a unity of its own, then all that surrounds it would be unheeded, and the results of this concentration will be that we have at once the feeling that the experience is ours owing to the mechanical memory, and also not ours but impersonal owing to the silence of all the usual associations.

It is out of this analysis of the self that the solution springs, and that solution can be best understood by consideration of a difficulty which one of the characters in the story brings forward. It is this. The sensation which has just been described with its dual character, the feeling that it is ours and the feeling that it is impersonal, may give an experience of timelessness or eternity because the ordinary sequence of associated memories has been disturbed; but it is not clear why such an experience should claim to be privileged. It is just like any other experience and therefore it should justify itself and submit to criticism and under that criticism it may show itself just as illusory as the others, just as incapable as the others to authenticate for us a divine reality. The answer is curious; it claims to turn the question by saying it cannot be asked. Criticism is silenced because it is gagged. One can only ask the question to oneself if there happens to be a self to act as tribunal, and the state which has just been described is reached precisely by escaping away from that self. In the moment of the experience the self with all the old distinctions which have been woven by the memories and the associations have disappeared;

44

the critic is back in ordinary life; he is outside the experience. Is this faith which transcends reason as one of the hearers suggests? No, the men who cling to the doctrine of faith

hold that there is one, and only one, road to the absolute. I suggest that there is only one road out of it. They put their trust in a narrow path that leads to God. I put mine in anything that can bar the path that leads *Hither*. To them the all-important thing is a given faith, its greatest development and constant presence in us, a moral process which we have watched and which can be best described as the triumph of personality. By this they escape from the world. To me the world as usually thought of, with its fundamental opposition of subject and object, appears and disappears, blinks into and out of existence with one particular rhythm of thought. It disappears with the dissolution of self; and personality is merely one of the possible means by which the dissolution may be effected.

Thus out of scepticism comes the shining truth; everything we can think of may be doubted and from every position which we take up we can be routed. But mankind goes serenely on, for it does not place its trust in reason. Reason is the doubter, " but a thorough doubt conditions itself; it conditions the desecrator and measures his tether. . . . The faith which shall stand must be dragged from the vitals of doubt. It must be the disenthronement of the great doubter: reason." All the values, so long as criticism remains, are like soldiers in a rank; we must step outside them. *Nos numerus sumus*. We endow the end with the qualities proper to the instrument with which we have achieved them; the divine we claim to have attained is only the projection of our human artistry.

But there is another wine. . . . It cannot be asked for, for it has no name ; it cannot be offered, for no vessel will hold it ; it runs through the crystal of thought as brandy runs through ice. . . . Where then is my philosopher's stone, my magic pebble ? I have none. I have no secret. I have nothing. Only the sorrow of my wasted life, only something that overwhelms and stuns me to rest, something mighty enough to break away from me, perfect enough to need me no more, to shake me off and endure for ever. But not in me ; and only for ever because not in me. If I seek to retain it and mingle it again with my substance by egress from which it was divine, it forthwith loses its divinity. . . . We are full of immortality. But it dwells not in the beauty of our moral person ; it stirs and glitters in us under the crust of self, like a gleam of sirens under the ice, and any blow which breaks this crust brings us into the company of the eternal ones whom to feel is to be they. That blow you will surely strike somehow, you who live and die. The film you have spread you will likewise rend ; surely, surely, you must slip into heaven. There is no rule of divine conduct, no text-book of enchantments. Say if you will, that they are always the same, one under many forms. Call them disguises of the emancipator. This you may do, but you cannot prescribe to him the method of your emancipation. He tears the veil as he chooses, with dawn-rose fingers of adoration and fiery fingers of enthusiasm, but also with the scarlet band of passion and the livid hand of death.

In the concluding pages of *The Prison* there are set down some remarks which throw further light on the view I have tried to summarize. One is that the ideal is not concerned with the guidance of life. That belongs to a different plane altogether. Another is that the unity arrived at is one similar to that of a drama in which " contrasting, irreducible scenes are comprised ; an unspeakable unity that cannot be focused in thought ; if it could be there would be no drama but an illustrated aphorism like one of Æsop's fables." If we do admit a ruling principle it identifies religion and morality and this is to smudge religion, to produce an autocratic system of philosophy. He admits that he has nothing to offer those who are really convinced in the persistence of the individual self after death, though he adds that such a scheme will not satisfy everybody,

because there are people in whose opinion to identify in essence the good and the divine is not to raise the good but to lower the divine; people whose religious instinct—the instinct that cries in the question, " Why all this and what is there behind it ? "— will always demand that the whole mass of inner adjustments of the human group should be referred to another order of facts.

What then the Prisoner is thinking of are those moments of experience which interrupt the mechanism which fabricates the idea we have of ourselves and of a world distinct from us and around us. That is part of life and experience, but it does not exhaust them. All the " wonderful co-ordination of instincts within the individual, and of thoughts within systems, and of men within communities only registers half the wealth of life," and they are unable also to touch and desecrate those sacred revelations which steal upon us, which belong to every creature and make him participate in the glory of the eternal.

I have spent some time over the views of Brewster in *The Prison* because they contain almost all that is to be said on the side of those who look for some ideal beyond that of orthodox theism. There is no conscious scamping of difficulties, no conscious belittling of values. The Prisoner wants the very best and will not be content with any view which is partial, which does not explore the highest dreams and conceptions of which man is capable, and at the same time he is wise and generous enough to demand that what he offers must be within the reach of everybody, the toiling, suffering people as well as the connoisseurs in beauty. He objects to the orthodox theism and Christianity because they do not seem to give him the unity for which he is searching. Religion as expressed in Christianity appears to him to be one among a number of other interests which make up human life ; it is not all-inclusive ; it is one of those everyday experiences on a level in kind if not in degree with morality, science and business. For the sake of clearness we may illustrate his meaning by the well-known division of Croce of the activities of man into art and philosophy, economics and ethics. These four are separate and distinct, and though Croce tries to construct a unity he does so without attempting to remove their distinctiveness. Now Brewster feels that if the supreme unity and perfect experience is described in terms of one of these four, the result is bound to be disappointing, and, as he says, religion is reduced to ethics and suffers thereby. But this is not his only difficulty. He is puzzled throughout by the problem of truth, and this problem presents itself to him in this

48

way. He believed that our experience starts with a number of impressions without any unity and that it is only when memory gets to work that unity starts. In recollection various equalities and analogies are noticed and these are grouped and classified; the next step is to make a further abstraction, for just as dissimilarities were left out in the groupings, so too we now concern ourselves with the groupings in so far as they reveal to us some common law and some common design. Now in so acting, the part played by our organism increases while less and less food, so to speak, is needed from outside. Our organism had some share even in our first impressions, but this is quadrupled when we come to the later abstractions. Lastly we reach a final abstraction, an " all-underlying structure or an all-containing substance," and this is God under one name or another.

Now this being so the question arises, what is the worth of these constructions, what relation do they bear to the reality ? One answer is none that we can know of, and it does not matter, because they have a value in themselves. This is the answer of one of the listeners in *The Prison*, and it has some resemblance to the position taken up by certain Modernists. They have no wish to test them because they are rather the tests of all other experience and " the idea of giving them additional dignity by claiming that they are images of so-called realities, or of backing them up with historical events " does not appeal to them. But others seek a sign and

surely they are right. At least we must know whether
our ideal is as real as the world around us which hurts
and thwarts us and at times helps. It is more than an
hallucination, and our ideal must have at least that
degree of reality. Yet Brewster cannot see light along
this direction, and the source of his difficulty is this, that
whatever he constructs by the mechanism of his personality and his reason appears to be limited by the mechanism and to be open to criticism from the very same
reason which had invented it. It is an old difficulty.
It was felt dimly by the child who said that God first
made a place for Himself to stand upon and then created
the world. The philosopher formulates it when he
argues that reason cannot be criticized because one would
have to get outside reason in order to do it, and the
idealist uses it when he says that it is foolish to talk
about the unknowable because if there were such a
thing we could not possibly know about it ; to mention
it even is to bring it within knowledge. Brewster
therefore wants to find a present which is not the end
of the past and beginning of the future, an island which
does not float on any sea or belong to the world of
which he is part ; he must turn the light out if he is
to see what he looks like in the dark, he must have a
privileged place from which he can survey everything,
a place which clearly must not belong to the universe
he is surveying and relative to it. Such a search may
seem doomed to failure, and the answers he first proposes
to himself look like the attempt of a man to find eternity

by indefinitely extending the limits of space and time. The ordinary theories of religion are man-made, like radii issuing from the self. He yields therefore all along the line, and in his very defeat he claims to find his victory; for all does not disappear when he makes this surrender. What does go is the self-centred standpoint and the conflicts of doubt, and in place of these he touches reality which is at the same time his own and more than all he can contain. The happy isles are reached which cannot be found in any geographical chart. They have no relation with the ordinary world, and he has to be back in his routine world before a breath of criticism can be stirred; and in this world the immortal element in which he dwelt has disappeared. What he is at liberty to say about it is that there is such a region and that all share in it at some moments of their life, that it is therefore universal, and that there are these experiences which transcend thought and all its satellites.

In the process of summarizing and explaining these views the penetration of Brewster, the truth of much of his criticism and the high quality of his desire for a genuine ideal and unity have struck me afresh; and at the same time despite every effort to appreciate the concluding part which gives his solution I cannot but feel that it falls below expectation. Let us take first what is lasting and true in his analysis. He is surely right in his dissatisfaction with many of the pretended ideals he tries to make his own. We have already discussed the strength of the Stoic position and Brewster admirably illustrates its weakness by showing how to a man in prison it can bring only a sham consolation. The prison is indeed a theatre in which the true can be easily distinguished from the false, and it is, I suppose, because a merely social and temporal ideal such as that proposed by social reformers, by socialists and communists, would have nothing to give a prisoner with a life sentence, that its possibilities are not even considered. What he wants he tells us clearly when he says that " there is this inexplicable character of the days of our lifetime, that taken separately they may be such common ware as glass beads, threaded together they turn into precious pearls." This new aspect, this unity must come from some wondrous power within us, and a materialistic creed, even when it is dialectic, cannot provide the individual with such a unity. All doctrines which call upon us to work for the greatest pleasure of the greatest number and embody this ideal in some state which controls all the means of production and ensures peace by eliminating competition and fixing status, are external to the real problem of happiness. Happiness can be found only where the ideals dimly or vividly felt in art and morality and religion are brought together in some possible experience. This experience Brewster calls at times eternal to bring out its difference from all the ephemeral, everyday joys and sorrows of mankind. He is impelled to go behind the passing show, to measure what must needs be by the highest of his interior aspirations, and in so doing he is the echo and witness of a countless company of poets and philosophers and saints, in fact he is the voice of everyman.

Again when Brewster makes his prisoner doubt the evidence of this changing world and depicts him as troubled in his soul with a constant fear of illusion, he is, I think, reproducing a not uncommon experience. The unreflective, straightforward citizen of this world takes life as he meets it ; he has no taste for silence, he has no habit of tracing within himself the sources of his beliefs ; he is like the man of common sense who accepts the world of appearances and has no interest in the strange universe revealed by the scientists. But the philosopher and the dreamer, the poet and the saint are haunted by intimations of another world. Some seem to hear within themselves the sound of a machinery which weaves the patterns they thought were real ; others have a sense of frustration as if some hidden meaning in the objects of their experience ever eluded them ; they catch too the sound of themselves in what they had hoped to be genuine and external. All, as Brewster points out, are perplexed and disheartened by the waste of so much that is precious, by the swift passing of themselves, of friends and of what they hold dear, in the river of time. There is no unity, certainly no abiding unity ; only " the futile effort to collect into one hour of consciousness the infinite and conflicting aspects of reality . . . even as a child suddenly thrown among strangers might clasp desperately in his hand some little familiar object, precious simply because familiar, with a vague sense that he could not quite lose his identity as long as he clasped the toy." The ordinary and orthodox guides, in Brewster's opinion, attempt to save the situation by tightening up experience, stiffening it into codes and formulæ. But these are only abstractions which unify and reach immutability by sacrificing the richness of life, by getting rid of the variety of its contents. Hence they do not integrate; they do not offer any consummating experience. They do not take us beyond the workaday conceptions which were the original cause of our dissatisfaction.

His own escape and solution we have already seen. He ceases to hope that he or any man while performing on the stage can tell what is going on behind the scenes, and in this act of self-abnegation he finds release. Gone are the stage and the critical audience, and yet there is not the silence of death; something survives to which the relation of subject and object does not apply, nor consequently the self-criticism which accompanies all our normal human functioning. Here again there is something which corresponds vaguely with what a number of distinguished men have felt. Each in his expression uses his own terms for it, but what appears to be common is the awareness somehow that there are realities undreamt of in commonplace philosophies, that we are in touch or can get into touch with something which transcends the ordinary working of reason, that there may be special faculties within us to enable us to do so ; at any rate whether this latter be true or not our reason is too rough an instrument to be of much assistance. This is the reason why rationalism is never practised by humanity to the degree its disciples demand, why romance always returns in the history of civilization no matter how often it is turned out, why philosophies are invented in which imagination or intuition or mystic experience or feeling or an *élan vital* are made of primary importance, why seers and prophets and wizards with occult powers, why theosophies and forms of spiritual science have ever abounded. Mr. Middleton Murry can claim a goodly company in support of whatever is substantial in his views about art and religion, though they might well dislike the manner in which he expresses them and think that he has done his best to confuse the issues, and the Abbé Brémond has borrowed from Claudel an enlightening parable of the relations of what are called Animus and Anima. These are but instances of a universal and continuous inclination to seek beyond the reason for the password into all truth.

But if this inclination be justified by the fact that the world does not seem to progress without appeal to it, it does not follow that this inclination has been always correctly analysed. Writers and thinkers, even the best, are inclined to rush from one extreme to another, to grow tired with a philosophy or system and to seize upon some element within or without that system and exaggerate it beyond its due. This over-emphasis has been responsible for almost all the historical heresies, and the views which Brewster adopts concerning the self and memory and concerning the reason are, in fact, heresies ; they exaggerate a truth and so prevent him from arriving at a satisfactory solution. There lies behind his views, also, an imperfect philosophy which was all too current in the nineteenth century. He assumes " that our brain is fashioned, so to speak, in a series of strata, such that each successive stratum draws an abstract proof of the picture presented on the preceding one. And further that this march of increasing abstraction is the cause of our notion of Law and Unity, both moral and in nature." Now this assumption is really a false start and leaves a crack running through his entire building. The correction of it is so important and bears so directly on what will be said later about the existence and nature of God, that we must be quite clear about the mistake and the true view. This entails a more thorough examination into a philosophical question than many people may like, but we cannot afford to be hazy on this matter. Hasty assumptions and too easily accepted slogans are the cause of the widespread confusion of thought over what concerns us most nearly, and so we grow despondent about discovering any truth. Let me begin by laying down that all knowledge cannot be an assumption as it is so commonly said to be. We cannot have the idea of the relative without some absolute, no more than we can think of odd without even or concave without convex. The images and analogies of shifting sands, changes in science, defective instruments fail because they all refer to some particular sphere of knowledge or reality. We can talk of changing tides and seas because we measure them by something stationary, we can in accordance with the recent hypotheses and experiments in science introduce a theory of Relativity into the universe because we have a firmer apprehension of what is absolute by means of it ; we can even talk of Evolution in many branches of science so long as we do not make the whole of reality subject to this form of change. To do so would give the *coup de grâce* to evolution and everything else, for if there were nothing permanent and stable which suffered change, then each change would be totally different from what had been before ; there would be nothing left of what had been, no possibility, therefore, of comparison, and the thought of this is enough to give us a nightmare. Even Jack-in-the-Boxes, startling as they are, leave much unchanged, whereas complete changes would literally spring up out of nothing, bearing with them nothing of a past and flashing by an observer who also is so changed from one moment to another that he can have no memory, no record of a past experience.

It is no exaggeration therefore to say that the aim to do away with all absolute certainty is more ridiculous than the action of the man who saws the branch on which he is sitting. It is more like the picture of the coffin of the prophet suspended in mid-air with the magnetic forces withdrawn. Brewster cannot, then, mean what he says when he uses the word " assumption," and makes his prisoner resign all hope of escaping from genuine doubt. Certainly the introspective man can have moods when he is beset by a feeling of illusion and even his own self seems to be a puppet dangled by invisible strings and as unreal as a puppet show ; such moods come and go, and, as I hope to show later, it is possible through over-reflection to diffuse so artificial a light over the scene of personal experience and memory as to lose the sense of identity. Such an event is not so much a warrant for scepticism as evidence for the account of human nature and human thinking, with its subtle interconnection of spirit and matter, which has been given by an old and sane philosophy. Scepticism, as has been pointed out time and again, is necessarily self-contradictory, for the very assertion of it is swept into the gulf of darkness which it opens out.

Nor again can the denial of knowledge of an external world be maintained. We cannot stop half-way and say that our thoughts may have validity, but they may not give us any information of what is external to us. A statement cannot be about nothing, and it is absurd to suggest that we can spin an airy universe of our own out of our own spiritual bowels ; for we have nothing which we have not received ; we are empty without experience, and this is why Brewster and all who take after him do at least bring in " impressions " or sensations, and without knowing it they almost invariably introduce much more. For instance, Brewster speaks freely of the brain and the body and other persons, and how often have we seen the spectacle of a man explaining to his friend that he knows nothing but his own sensations or developing an argument in favour of the subjectivity of his own thought by an appeal to the physiological processes of the body and the brain! As a matter of fact, the drawbridge is down as soon as sensations and impressions are mentioned, for there must be something to make the impression, and this distinction between what is subjective and what is external implies some knowledge of reality however infinitesimal.

This inch of reality gained yields an ell, nay infinity, for to tell the truth the opponent of theism has lost the game by giving away that one real pawn. Once we are out of the world of illusion, of impenetrable darkness in knowledge, once we see land, no matter how foggy the outlook, we can go forward without a single serious check. Of course, the land of reality may contain all kinds of wonders of which we may not know the existence. Of course, too, we may not be able to know it by intimate acquaintance, but we can tell what is " nor'-nor'-west and how the wind can be in the south and remark on the difference of a hawk from a handsaw." In other words, we have got the hang of reality ; knowing one real we can say something about any real thing, just as if we know what a flower is from having come across one, we are not completely at a loss when a traveller from far places or an antiquarian were to tell us about varieties with which we have not the slightest acquaintance. But, I have no doubt a sceptical friend will reply, the cases are not alike and it is absurd to claim that by jumping off the bank into a pool of water one has discovered the bottom of the sea and all that the ocean contains. It is, I admit, a justifiable objection, as the parallel of the flower does over-simplify the problem. All flowers, however many subdivisions of species we make, belong to one genus, whereas there are more things in reality than even the Walrus could think of if he talked to the Carpenter all day. Everything that exists or will exist or can exist falls under the general appellation of something; all the physical objects of the universe, their colour as well as their shape, time and thoughts swifter than time; and if this is so, have we not just wasted our time in calling them all by one title, seeing that they are so totally and immeasurably different?

There are many philosophers who ridicule this method of approach which has just been given and criticized, and they score with the crowd which is easily made to think it stupid to try to derive our knowledge of reality out of the minimum of knowledge given to us by the word " real " or " thing." True, we must not expect too much of it, and if we had to stop there we should not be better off than the baby which makes its first efforts at thought and language. Nevertheless, we cannot despise this little token, the first symbol of the mighty power of intelligence and the sure evidence that

God has made us in His own image and given the world
and all it contains as the prize of our intellectual striving.
It may be a minimum, but it is better than nothing.
There is a modern school of thinkers who, seeing that
it is the enemy of their scepticism, have tried to destroy
its significance by calling it a misleading expression, but
they do not observe that it cannot be totally misleading
since we cannot do without it; indeed, if we tried to do
so, then we should be unable even to criticize it, for
our criticism would not be real.   Moreover, they suppose
that this initial statement, that what we are perceiving
or thinking of is something, is at best a scaffolding or
makeshift which, as our knowledge develops, we can
discard. A child may call a ball and a dog both
" thing "; later, it is suggested, the child will learn their
true names and so something about the two objects.
But what is forgotten in this view is that even when the
child knows the two things for what they are, they still
remain as much as ever two things, and there is not the
slightest inaccuracy in so continuing to describe them,
and if every possible information about them were
acquired so that we knew them better than we do ourselves, they would still not cease to be the two things.
And the reason is obvious, for by so describing them
we are referring to that in them which remains identical,
no matter what differences are found later to exist, an
identity, or at least a likeness, which permits us to move
from any piece of terra firma, from any object to a survey
of the universe from end to end.   This little mica flake,

therefore, of knowledge is the foundation and condition of the great mountains of science and philosophy which the ages have constructed, and has the right to be considered of the greatest importance.

Having established this we can now go on to point out the other defects in the account which Brewster gives. One obvious result of his defective theory of knowledge is his unwillingness to be impressed by his own argument for God in the passage I have already quoted on page 41 about the voucher and the warrant behind reality. The argument has a certain validity once it is recognized that the conceptions of the mind are true of the external world. The form in which he expresses it may give cold comfort to those who desire a living and loving God, and indeed it would need correction, but if we are content with the crumbs that fall from the table instead of expecting from human knowledge a feast of divinity, the cold statement of fact will bring more satisfaction than myriad experiences none of which can justify its authenticity. So many want to persuade themselves that their soul is a windjammer full sail for eternity, but if our condition is that of a submarine we must be content with a periscope. Brewster, indeed, is so anxious not to exaggerate our condition, that he dares not trust his mind and his self and he runs away from his own shadow. In his opinion the self is nothing more than a locus or meeting-point of memories. Strange as such a view may appear to those who have taken themselves for granted, it is not far from the truth. The awareness that we have of ourselves is dependent on our body, our senses and memory. Not that it is constituted by them, for we are more than we can contain in the thought of ourselves. The self that is ours as subject of all our activities and dispositions and the self that is object of consciousness are different as the representation from the reality. Hence we speak of men not knowing themselves, the fools, the coxcombs, the Malvolios believe in a portrait of themselves which does not correspond with the truth. In so far, however, as they attach this portrait to real facts of their history with the help of memory, they have of course a modicum of truth in their reflections on themselves. But even this may be affected, for the memory is partly at least physical, and like the body it may be attacked. When the memory snaps like a reel at the cinema the human being may lose hold in part of his self-identity. He suffers then from what has been called a split personality. The same phenomenon may be due to an unexpected change in the condition of the body, for we do not suspect how much the unity in our self-consciousness and in our representations of self is due to that all-overish feeling given to us by the unified sensations and sensibility of the body, which is called technically conæsthesia. Such evidence as this would appear at first sight to tell in favour of a phenomenal self, but in reality the correct interpretation supports the orthodox view. The data just given which could be multiplied, if taken on their face value do turn into a heresy, the one-sided view.

Even granting that the self we represent to ourselves on the object side of consciousness is dependent on the above-mentioned factors, that does not dispose of the self which is in fact the subject and agent of all the changes which go on in consciousness. We may never be able to glimpse its full reality in this life, but we are aware of it as that which is the accompaniment of all our activities and as their source. That is to say we have to correct somewhat the analysis of the self-as-object by adding that we as the subject and ourselves as object, the nominative and the accusative, mutually help out the understanding of each other. We learn by reflecting on our nature that we are one permanent being with a unity which holds together as our own spirit and body and expresses itself in the various activities of thinking, desiring, moving. The idea we have of ourselves is affected by our moods and our physical condition, and it may divide up into departments of the various functionaries within us. "If you are called on suddenly to say who you are, you think of your name, of your reputation, of your work, of your friends, of your abode, perhaps of your club or of the Church to which you belong." But normally we can compare these different aspects of ourselves and normally, too, we can pass a fair judgment on ourselves ; at least we can be aware in moments of decision, if we take heed, of the reasons of our choice, and by so doing we commit the whole of ourselves to the act we have in mind. And we can do this because we are not only aware of ourselves as an object of thought but as thinking and willing ; we can see the shadow, and more than the shadow of our real self athwart the act, crouching to its spring. And this is why, despite all that the opponents of personality and human nature say, man goes on in the present age as ever before sure that he is one and the same the whole of his life despite all the changes which take place within him, sure also that he is responsible to himself because he is director and judge of his conduct. And if this should be thought not enough to prove that man is more than a seat of memories there is the convincing proof that all the different departmental selves are his, and unified in him in a way which makes them belong to him solely for his weal or woe. If by some illness of the mind his person seems torn asunder for a while, the fragments still belong to the being who has that mind and body and they can be reassembled together, when health is restored, as the memories and history of one being.

I have insisted on this emendation in the analysis of the self as given by Brewster because it furnishes us once more with the principles which enable us to understand both why searchers after perfection, like Morgan and Brewster and many another, tend to look beyond reason and the self for their ideal, and how the Christian teaching takes over what they say without their shortcomings and exaggerations. They do not comprehend the philosophy of Christianity and because of this they are inclined to look for some ideal which is superior. Thus they fail to observe that both in its philosophy of knowledge and in its theory of the self, this teaching first states the dignity of man with his limitations, and it is only when this lesson has been driven in that it lights up the sky from end to end with beauty. The pagan suppliants of perfection want the award immediately ; they would turn the god Pan into a figure of untroubled joy and they are bound to shut their eyes to the changing moods of the forest and earth which we have for habitation. By contrast the Christian creed is painted in sombre and puritanical colours, as the enemy of the body and of the senses and happy feasting. Some versions of Christianity may justify this reproach, but it is a parody of the traditional and orthodox theology. There is present in Christianity a sombre note, and there are periods of the ecclesiastical year which are given over to discipline and fasting. These, however, must be seen in perspective, and it would be quite wrong to think that Christianity regards the world as evil and the joy of the senses as a sin. The real and vital difference between the Christian conception of life and those I have been portraying is that it views this life as only the seed-plot of an eternal flowering. The three score and ten years are a preparation, a time of growth and testing, a moment taken out of eternal life for man to say yea or nay to the proposal of divine love, and it is man's part to be faithful to truth and goodness before he realizes their consummation in experience. We have now the foretaste and substance of things hoped for, but eye hath not seen nor ear heard

what things are prepared for those who believe and love
in absence.

This is not the place to develop the philosophy contained in the Christian creed. That may come later.
For the moment we must concentrate on the failure of
all contrary ideals to provide a substantial faith. They
look to this life for completeness and, discouraged by
the prospect given by human reason, they jettison it and
look elsewhere. I have tried to show that they underrate
the power of reason, while admitting that the truth it
gives us is disappointing, and this because we are still
travellers and have not reached the end. The alternative,
that we can find happiness in this life, is a will-o'-the-
wisp. The hero of *The Fountain* failed and Brewster
fails, and it has always seemed to me astonishing that
moralists do not realize how vain is their effort to make
a complete ethics out of the data of human life. Almost
all the modern writers on this subject ignore the possibility of our immortal destiny. There is indeed one
notable exception, A. E. Taylor. His book, *The Faith
of a Moralist*, is a noble plea for an alliance between
religion and morality and for a life of immortality. But
with this one notable exception modern books on morals
ignore the after-life, and for the most part they are stuck
by a problem, the relation of the right to the good. By
the good they mean happiness and by right duty, and
the difficulty is to see how doing one's duty can lead to
or be measured by happiness. Clearly there is no completely satisfactory answer to this difficulty within the

limits of this life. As one of the greatest of all philosophers pointed out, the perfect life in this world is a
haphazard affair. We require so many gifts and so many
opportunities for exercising them, and it would be the
rarest thing in the world for one man to enjoy all these
opportunities, to have good health, bodily possessions,
good friends and both intellectual and moral qualities.
Even supposing they were all present for a long time,
it would not follow that the lucky individual would be
satisfied. We can be sure indeed that he would be far
from satisfied. And as to the vast majority of the
human race, they are apparently to look on and rejoice
that one at any rate has been the darling of fortune.
Meantime they have to labour and sweat, to suffer illness
and misfortune, to be misrepresented, sow for others to
reap, to receive praise for things ill-done and punishment
or contempt for what was meritorious. And not only
is this their fate, but judged by the standards of this
world the value of their work and the meaning of their
existence are left a complete mystery. When we have
taken away the vision of a life beyond the grave in which
the intention will be judged as more important than the
result, in which too a purpose will be seen to have lifted
much of what is done by nameless people from futility
to significance, what answer can be made to the land-
less poor when they claim to possess even by force all
that can be grabbed in the few animal years that are
theirs ?

Poets and idealists may continue to paint life in rosy

colours and social reformers kindle passion by dwelling on the manifest inequality of life in modern society, but neither has succeeded in making their medicine into a universal cure or in removing the obvious distresses and evils which stand in the way of individual as well as universal happiness. Long ago Pascal, having stared into the face of nature and found there a hideous blank countenance if God be not alive, defined the alternatives of theism and atheism and said that we must wager. " We run carelessly to the precipice," he tells us, " after we have put something before us to prevent us seeing it." But if we open our eyes we see that

we sail within a vast sphere ever drifting in uncertainty, driven from end to end. When we think to attach ourselves to any point and to fasten to it, it wavers and leaves us ; and if we follow it, it eludes our grasp, slips past us, and vanishes for ever. This is our natural condition, and yet most contrary to our inclination ; we burn with desire to find solid ground and an ultimate sure foundation whereon to build a tower reaching to the Infinite. But the whole groundwork cracks, and the earth opens to abysses.

Hide therefore the fact as we may, we are in a desperate state, for " we are something and not everything. The nature of our existence hides from us the knowledge of first beginnings which are born of the Nothing ; and the littleness of our being conceals from us the sight of the Infinite." Beaten and stunned by thoughts such as these we have to choose between the acceptance of a God and the denial of Him. And there is no burking of this choice, for willy-nilly we decide by our conduct one way or the other.

Yes; but you must wager. It is not optional. You are embarked. Which will you choose then? Let us see. Since you must choose, let us see which interests you least. You have two things to lose, the true and the good; and two things to stake, your reason and your will, your knowledge and your happiness, and your nature has two things to shun, error and misery. Your reason is no more shocked in choosing one rather than the other, since you must of necessity choose. This is one point settled. But your happiness? Let us weight the gain and the loss in wagering that God is. Let us estimate these two chances. If you gain you gain all; if you lose you lose nothing. Wager, then, without hesitation that he is . . . " That is very fine. Yes, I must wager; but I may perhaps wager too much."—Let us see. Since there is an equal risk of gain and of loss, if you had only to gain two lives, instead of one, you might still wager. But if there were three lives to gain, you would still have to play (since you are under the necessity of playing), and you would be imprudent, when you are forced to play, not to chance your life to gain three at a game where there is an equal risk of loss and gain. But there is an eternity of life and happiness. And this being so, if there were an infinity of chances, of which one only would be for you, you would still be right in wagering one to two, and you would act stupidly, being obliged to play, by refusing to stake one life against three at a game in which out of an infinity of chances, there is one for you, if there were an infinity of an infinitely happy life to gain. But there is here an infinity of an infinitely happy life to gain, a chance of gain against a finite number of chances of loss, and what you stake is finite. It is all divided; wherever the infinite is and there is not an infinity of chances of loss against that of gain, there is no time to hesitate, you must give all. And thus, when one is forced to play, he must renounce reason to preserve his life, rather than risk it for infinite gain, as likely to happen as the loss of nothingness.

The wager, as Pascal puts it, is worked out subtly, and we need not follow him its full length to see the point he is making. We can indeed formulate it in a different way as follows: Leave aside the certainty which can be attained by rational proof of God, since this proof leaves us still palpitating in the dark of our present condition. A far-off event, no matter how much evidence is brought by our friends of its truth, leaves us hesitating when our present circumstances seem to tell against it. Try then another tack, and consider whether it is worth the risk in deciding for it. If God does not exist, then what is our position? Much of what we think and have in mind to do seems to be left as it was. The world has not suddenly changed colour. Our friends are still beside us, our occupations still provide for us their natural interest, the future may be lucky. There are plenty of acquaintances who never think of God and are, to all appearances, content and making enough out of this temporal life. There are, too, many high-minded men who hold that duty and value are not affected one way or the other by theories about ultimates; justice must be done even if there be no God and an ideal can ennoble a man even if he believe in no hereafter.

All the same few can be persuaded that questions about the end of life are a pure waste of time and that beliefs make no difference to conduct. Historical precedents go to show that a culture goes to pieces when belief declines, and in answer to the objection just raised it must be pointed out that the present generation is still living on the tradition of a Christian civilization. The modern agnostic is benefiting by the ideals which have soaked into the minds of men, and now that they are beginning to evaporate we are face to face with moral disturbances from which earlier generations were saved. The widespread dishonesty in civil life, the decline in modesty and respect for age, parents and all authority, the growing license which besmirches true love, and the habit of suicide, these and many other phenomena are causing alarm even in the ranks of those who reck little of religion. And we have little or no evidence of the end to which we are moving because never before has there been a society or culture which ignored God completely. We have no warrant therefore for saying that the lack of ultimate sanctions will make no difference to ideals and conduct; all the evidence there is points to a directly opposite conclusion. So frightening is the outlook to some leading freethinkers that they advocate the retention of values and ideas, in which they do not believe, in order to check the coming materialization of body and soul. It would look therefore as if the dropping of a heavenly pilot does make a vital difference to the State, though the change may at first be imperceptible, and many good men may carry on a tradition of high endeavour and moral purpose.

I cannot believe, however, that even the most worthy atheist can be called wise. It is the prerogative of man to " look before and after," to seek for a synoptic vision of life and to be satisfied with nothing but the best. That is why the great reformers of society, those who have been accepted by mankind as its saints and heroes, have been discontented with vulgarity and temporal successes and oppressed by a sense of the vanity of much that is held dear. They make explicit what is near to the heart of most of us. As it has been well said, the only genuine ideas are " the ideas of the shipwrecked. All the rest is rhetoric, posturing, farce. He who does not really feel himself lost, is lost without remission ; that is to say, he never finds himself, never comes up against his own reality." The man who settles himself comfortably in the present is like to those who dwell on the slope of a volcano, or to men in a dug-out in a moment of reprieve who know not for what they are fighting or whether they have any chance of survival. They live in a fool's paradise. Ortega y Gasset is surely right when he declares in *The Revolt of the Masses* that

human life, by its very nature, has to be dedicated to something, an enterprise glorious or humble, a destiny illustrious or trivial. We are faced with a condition, strange but inexorable, involved in our very existence. On the one hand, to live is something which each one does of himself and for himself. On the other hand, if that life of mine, which only concerns myself, is not directed by me towards something, it will be disjointed, lacking in tension and in "form." In these years we are witnessing the gigantic spectacle of innumerable human lives wandering about lost in their own labyrinths, through not having anything to which to give themselves. . . . Given over to itself, every life has been left empty, with nothing to do. And it has to be filled with something, it invents frivolities for itself, gives itself to false occupations which impose nothing intimate, sincere. To-day it is one thing, to-morrow another, opposite to the first. Life is lost at finding itself all alone. Mere egoism is a labyrinth. This is quite understandable. Really to live is to be directed towards something, to progress towards a goal. The goal is not my motion, not my life, it is something to which I put my life and which consequently is outside it, beyond it. If I decide to walk alone inside my own existence, egoistically, I make no progress. I arrive nowhere.

Ortega y Gasset in the passages quoted and in his book does not specify whether the alternatives he so contrasts are those of religion and atheism, but there can be no doubt that his language is applicable to them. If we exclude the theistic and personal explanation of the universe and our own life, then we are left with a dark mystery both at the origin and at the end. We have too no guarantee that the good we try to accomplish will bear any fruit, and for all we know we may be engaged on a futile campaign. The whispering voice within which asks us continually, Why court pain and trouble, why make distinctions between the sensual and the spiritual, the unselfish and the selfish, what doth it profit to be patient and modest and humble, to quicken the good in others? cannot be stilled. If there be no purpose in human existence which embraces the whole of life, then we must take everything at its surface value and there is nothing further to be revealed; and if we be ignorant whether there be a purpose, then for all we know the good that we think we do may be destructive. To tamper with a machine of which we know next to nothing generally ends in our wrecking it, and the human organism and character are far more complicated than any machine. As it is, with all the experience of the past, social reformers cannot agree

as to the best way of building the city of man ; some
cry for more freedom, others for more discipline, and
no one can dare prophesy whether by sparing the
criminal we do more ultimate good than harm, whether
charity be not a social crime, praise a stimulant of
vanity and pride, and truth-telling less beneficial in the
long run than lying.

There are some who will remain unmoved by all
these threats of pessimism which await an atheistic
philosophy, and it is strange how little what is afar off
whether in time or space affects us. Like the woman
at the lecture we are relieved to hear that the lecturer
prophesied the end of the world not in fifty million
years but in two hundred million. She felt that there
was more breathing space for her ! In fact, however,
the relative imminence of the end does not affect its
reality, though it does change our emotional reactions,
as the guests of Belshazzar discovered. Death is an
end and to those who do not believe in God a final
end; they need not fear any more the heat of the sun
nor the furious winter's rages, but they have gone to
no home and they will receive no wages. Dust is their
destiny and possibly the entail of four planks. By a
pathetic fallacy we endow them with a spurious immortality ; the survivors will not at first speak ill of them,
and grateful friends may try to retain their memory,
as though they were still sensitive to praise and blame.
But we have only to think of the civilizations of which
we do not know the name of a single member to see

that fame is a poor substitute for personal survival and that nature is not provident like God and mindful of its children. Brewster's ideal draws near to this fallacy in the concluding pages of *The Prison*, though the lack of substance is hidden by the beauty of the description. The soul surrenders its identity but persists in the ideal state which is beyond rational statement. Unfortunately beyond rational statement must mean here what is unintelligible, and so we are faced with two alternatives to the theist ideal, one in which we shut our eyes to all ultimate issues and blindly hope for the best of lives without any absolute standards, without any security against the possible malignity of fate—and with this bankrupt policy we address the world around us of happy and unhappy beings. And the other alternative is to take refuge in some mysterious experience about which we can say nothing save that it tries to unite together the loss of all individuality and the possession of what we would most dearly love, a unity therefore which so far as one can see is really the setting side by side of two contradictories.

I have tried to guess the alternatives to the theist position, and it would have been easy to make the picture much blacker. I have refrained from doing so because I might run the risk of appearing to exaggerate. Let, however, those who have not thought of contemplating the necessary consequences of the denial of God do so sincerely, not shirking the argument and not duping themselves with fancied ideals and dreams which cannot come true. They will find that they have made themselves bedfellows of many an illusion and that the spirit they have chosen for companion is a devil with a whip as stinging as a scorpion. By some freak of the mind denial can give pleasure and take on the semblance of something positive. But in escaping from one habitation we do not find ourselves in a free country, the lords of infinite space. The first breath of freedom may make us think that this is so, but in reality we are trespassing on some other land, and we must look about us to discover where we are. The old name for the place where God does not reign is Pandemonium, and it is the duty of the atheist to enlighten himself and others as to the nature of this place and not cozen others by spending his time in negative criticism. We are so apt to forget that we must wager, that the old adage about the frying-pan and the fire holds true, that a change of view is often attractive because of its novelty and that this is its only attraction. Moreover, we want everything at once ; we cannot wait and suffer in order to win a far-off but lasting prize, and so, ignoring our condition, we deceive ourselves with the expectation of some Utopia, where we can live the life of the happy innocents or the recluse or the mystic, or make a Soviet Republic where all will be able, like the lovers in the fairy tale, to live happily for ever afterward. Truth is better than such fictions, and in the much misunderstood Christian teaching no quick returns are promised but a vigorous novitiate

77

admirably adapted to the weakness and strength of human nature and at the end a richness of life which embraces all the best in the hasty ideals already mentioned and surpasses them as the notes of the real nightingale outvie all clock-work imitations. All that is to follow will go to prove this, but as a fitting end to this chapter it will be well to indicate how this can come about.

The ideals which have been set forward as alternatives to that of Christian theism fail like the guesses of men lost in a mist in an unknown country. Or again they can be described as an attempt to make a fine day without the sun.

Again and again the same songs of joy and art and invulnerable strength are sung and the singers follow the same course; the theme slows down as youthful exuberance is quelled by experience, and the note of a stoic or mystic faith is heard, which in turn yields with time to pessimism, or, please God, to truth. A recent book called *Jack Robinson*, by George Beaton, sets it out once more in language which will recur in these pages and as a kind of choral accompaniment because of its beauty and sincerity. The boy hero starts with romance and quickly surrenders to life as he finds it, wrapping himself up in a cloak of fortitude. But this could not last.

I still continued to fly on my turrets the banner of Stoic inflexibility conducting to a sage's happiness and in moments of self-reproach or depression to judge the world, which did not accept these ideals, with proportionate severity. But in practice I had totally abandoned it as altogether too crude for my requirements and was busy pointing my mind against more subtle and more genuine issues.

What these issues were and what the new comforting solution must be can be easily guessed. He wished, like Brewster, to assure himself of the greatest possible number of moments of joy in the apprehension of beauty, and the means

lay in the direction of Science and Art. . . . Art gives us organized and precise impressions, it develops them (in the case of music and literature) by a process of analysis, which by engaging at first only the attention ends by greatly amplifying the total emotion. . . . Works of Science too, built up though they are upon that part of experience most repugnant to and different from the æsthetic moment, the largest common factors in the operations of the Universe, the things that recur minutely and monotonously in it, constitute for those who make the effort to approach them the same perpetual fountain of beauty.

But already in his experience the hero recognizes the difficulty of reconciling the high and perhaps rare moments of true artistic enjoyment with the rest of life. For a time the answer seemed to lie in a still more resolute loyalty to Art, in

a formula by which I could co-ordinate and employ the rations daily allotted to me of energy and beauty. . . . I did not know then that the only solution to such problems—the only means of avoiding a destructive choice, the only means of extracting from each experience what is significant in it, the only means then of building up a world or system that is entirely expressive and does not consist like the one we are born into of patches of meaning set in insignificance and nonsense, lies in Art. Art is the sole resource of those poor and helpless imbeciles to whom the gods with their insidious malice have poured out too rich a cup of life-sustaining nectar.

Such are the hopes of this young traveller and in time he will find, like the rest, that he is only preparing for himself disillusionment. The discovery that he too, like so many others, has failed because he has miscalculated the nature and powers of man I will quote later, but already what he has experienced reinforces the truth that man is in a state of transition all the days of his life and that there is no moment when he can say of himself, Here is my tabernacle, here the Ultima Thule of my advance. His body has its seasons and decays, and the mind owing to its intimate connection with the body is fresh and most energetic after adolescence. But the life of the spirit is only then at its beginning and each one is well aware that he can grow indefinitely in virtue and wisdom. Nor will the soul ever be at rest. As the years pass they bring with them some victories and many defeats; they drive in the lesson of impotence and frustration and leave a sense of failure, our failure in reflection to have become all that we might have been if only we had made the best of all the opportunities offered to us. Those philosophers, therefore, who have spoken of the life of man upon this earth as a period of preparation or trial or moulding of the soul or journeying or apprenticeship are right, and it follows that we cannot expect a state of bliss in this life; we can only conjecture from our embryonic condition what such a perfection will be like. In the meantime we must be content with what we are and have and make the best of it. Now the complaint of Brewster and all the enemies of reason is that it is such a dilatory and inadequate assistant, a mere handmaid whereas we should like it to be the mistress. Still it is of no use to kick against the goad, and if we have to use crutches to be morally good, to accept the discipline of others, to allow for the wretched state of our nerves and stomach and brain, to go to school and learn with trouble and tedium the elements of mathematics and the grammar of different languages, to purify our bad taste in music and poetry, to take time before we master other people's thoughts, well, that is the lot of every human creature, the one royal road to victory. That all the lasting triumphs of man in thought have been gained by the mind which has submitted to this discipline, no one can deny. Certainly there must be added the flash of genius, the startling insight into dark places, and when man is at his best he is not merely a thinking machine but a person with desires and sensitive bodily equipment and a memory stored with fabulous treasures. But the fact remains that he cannot do without his reason, that all successes have been gained by means of it and that these successes and the very nature of thinking itself prove conclusively that truth cannot be wooed by any other means. So if we eat but of the crumbs of reality, if the little light vouchsafed to us is surrounded with darkness, let us, for heaven's sake, take what truth we may instead of forsaking it all for the ghost of an illusion. Small beginnings may have a joyous end, and in our greediness we may lose all and suffer eternal frustration. What we can learn we have now to see.

CHAPTER II

THE GRANDEUR OF THEISM

SO far I have been attempting to describe some of the alternative ideals to that of Christian theism and some of my readers may complain that I have said nothing about the form of life which would give them the greatest pleasure. But how am I to know what that is ? I have taken two statements, the one by Charles Morgan and the other by Brewster, because more than one person has drawn my attention to the former and the second seems to me personally to be as wise and noble an effort to think out some supreme form of happiness as can be found in modern literature. The philosophers try to make a list of the various alternatives possible, but they have no means of telling or relating the variety of different forms which the ideal will take in various individuals' thoughts. The poor sempstress who sighed for rest and nothing else but rest is bound to formulate her desires differently from, shall we say, an Oscar Wilde or D. H. Lawrence. Keats, for whom truth is beauty, and Marx, for whom it is economic equality, are separated by an abyss, and many of my readers may be clamorous for some favourite plan and ideal of their own—not always their own, for they may have been inspired by a novel or essay they have just read or some hidden loyalty. There are moods during which we are disciples of Omar Khayyam, times when we are without rest and long to set out, like Ulysses, to seek better worlds or travel without end. There are some who are short-sighted and live only for the next excitement or step in advance, as the visitor at the Vatican who remarked that "being Pope was not so bad, but he did not see what it led to"; and there are others more long-sighted, who regard all as waste of time until they achieve what they want. The writers of the present day seem to be over-conscious of the herd life which masses of people lead and of the glass houses with glazed panes behind which the older generation of the supposedly wise sat. Poor wiseacres! They are told now by their young friends that they must stop their chatter, that what the world needs is a return to primitive instincts and the many-hued life of the senses. A murrain on the pedagogues who have kept the children inside on a summer's day, and so by words and by words our life is to be coaxed into being a continual summer.

How then am I to proceed when in this fair of the world everyone is calling out the superlative quality of their own wares? Well, he indeed would be foolish who expected to convert all to his point of view. When young we take for granted that truth will easily prevail, that people have only to be told of their mistakes and of what is best for them and that straightway they will arise from their errors and dance to the piping of wisdom. Yet the wisest of men and the wisdom of God both suffered the loss of their lives at the hands of those they would fain have helped, and it is with despair almost that we watch as we grow older so many who insist on choosing folly as their lot and walking into the city of their own damnation. In a book on the end of life and communion with God it would seem most fitting to furnish oneself with arguments of compelling logic, and were man what he so often claims to be, namely, a highly rational being, such a procedure would be imperative. But books of philosophy have stirred the world less than romances and poetry, and personal experience is more decisive than a hundred syllogisms in *barbara*. And it is for this reason that I have chosen to mingle argument with an appeal to what we most want and to rely on some of those wants being sufficiently universal to evoke a common response and assent.

It is time now to approach the theistic ideal and to examine its claims to supremacy. As evidence for its supremacy I think two tests can be applied, one that it is the highest of ideals and the second that it is the most complete. As an immediate argument in favour of its completeness, there is the fact that it gives us intellectual satisfaction. This assertion may sound surprising because we are so often told that theism is a pious aspiration, a belief beyond or against reason and supported by religious experience. Just as science can reduce music to "the dragging of the tail of a dead horse over the intestines of a dead cat," so it can make of religion the fumes of an intoxicant rising to the head, but since those who are blest with a musical ear or religious sense swear that this is not all and that they have experienced something ineffable, there may, so the conclusion runs, be something beyond reason. The sober-minded will say that this is a caricature, and perhaps it is, but the fact remains that many, even of the sober-minded, have been persuaded that the leaders of the theist camp do not rely on reason. So far from this being the truth the opposite generally holds. An atheist of my acquaintance once argued with some vigour that coherence was a necessary characteristic of truth, but he maintained that the undeniable presence of evil in the universe made belief in God impossible. When taxed with the difficulty that then he must fall back on an ultimate incoherence and give up truth, he admitted the former but refused to surrender the latter, and as an escape from the difficulty he protested that theism was in the like quandary. Such are the straits of all who reject God. Now it is an undeniable fact that the mind will never be satisfied until it has some explanation of the contents of experience and the world around it, and explanation requires some kind of unity or unification. We are essentially tidy-minded; we cannot leave things higgledy-piggledy. No sooner does the child begin to reason than it occupies itself with the fascinating game of asking questions, and every pursuit of man has the same purpose, to know the why and wherefore of this seemingly connected and disconnected world of events without and within. Nothing that appears to happen at random can satisfy us, whether we watch a game for the first time or a picture or car or train, and fortunately for our health of mind we all of us take for granted that the world outside us and our own bodies has meaning and is governed by laws, however obscure. I say "fortunately" because were we once to suspect that all was not well with our assumption we should rapidly become eligible for a lunatic asylum.

There is no need to develop this assertion at length. I know that philosophers at times like to tell us that we know nothing about causes, that knowledge is a by-product of our animal industry, and similar nonsense. Not a single one of these philosophers dreams of living his ugly fairy tale, and we must remember that philosophers are particularly prone to live in a cloud-cuckoo land and, like children, to enjoy sailing kites. They have against them every particle of experience the human race has ever possessed. The whole system of our education gives them the lie, and all thought from the primitive essays down to the massive constructions of modern science springs from the ineradicable desire and hope of man to know the nature of reality. Now there are many provinces of knowledge, and however distinct they may be we simply cannot endure the possibility that they are entirely unconnected. We must have unity at any price, and in the past many have sacrificed truth in their determination to have a unity. Wise man after wise man has with Procrustean ruthlessness cut the universe to fit his idea of unity. Looking over the past we may be tempted to wonder at times how famous thinkers could have been so foolish. Young men grow impatient when they have to spend hours deciphering what seem to them dead and absurd philosophies. It is worth pointing out that quite as much folly can be found in contemporary thought, and the reason for the never-ceasing scribbles, this unceasing pother about nature and life, is the insatiable craving of man for unity and truth.

Now theism supplies the answer and the only possible answer. The unity cannot just be a census in which, like Palestine in the reign of Augustus, everything is numbered. Equality and fraternity, again, cannot be the principle of unity; there is order and dependence; there is quality as well as quantity; there are degrees of power, of beauty and of goodness. A vague Pantheism, while it bears witness to the conviction of some unity, is no better than Pandemonium, and, as we know, Pandemonium defines the condition of the damned. The Absolute is another word which has been coined to fix the imagination and give peace to the mind, but if this be no more than the convex side of that global universe we picture or the form to the content or animating principle of the body of our knowledge, we are deluding ourselves with words and we are back again at the beginning with the stark universe confronting us. Many, as I have suggested, give up the struggle here and try, as it were, to cork the ocean by a proud assertion of ignorance. They think such ignorance is the highest knowledge and manage by calling black white to befool the multitudes for a while. Aristotle, in one of his rare splendid phrases, remarked, "On this principle hang the heavens and the earth," and we need not bother about the exact context of his remark to gather from it the truth that philosophy cannot, any more than the universe itself, hang suspended in mid-air. We need a principle which does not, like a light-house beacon, now shine and now suffer eclipse, which is stable with unvarying strength, giving and never spent and complete with all the scattered and finite glories of the universe we know. Here we have unity and order and the ultimate satisfaction of the intellect.

Now some will be sure to say that this is nothing but a hard saying clothed in facile words, and even were the intellect pleased with such a myth, this God is far from Him whom religion recognizes. Not so. There are conditions which must hold true of the God who is discovered by us in the world outside and in ourselves. Among them one is that I cannot be part of God or anyone else or of nature, and a second is that all the perfections in nature, in others and in myself must run together in some supreme unity and be caught up into some beauty which neither I nor friends nor nature could ever attain. I know well that poets and phil-

osophers in their train have spoken as if I could become
one with nature and sink or rise into godhead, and
love amongst men and women has chosen the language
of identification. But close as we can come to nature
and to friends there is an abyss no one can cross ; the
solitude of the self. If nature be not a phantom, if there
be anything real there, then it lifts itself up against me.
It may be mine, it is not I. *Quisque suos patimur manes* ;
I cannot be multiplied or diffused ; I cannot change
into another and be myself ; I cannot die and live.
And if this be so with an unresponsive nature, much
more so is it with friends. They and I, indeed, have
intercommunication, and love and knowledge bring us
far closer than nestlings that are warm beneath their
mother's wing. By a permissible exaggeration the
happiness of such love can be described in terms of
full union ; but it is not identity. Two different persons still inhabit the same world, differing not merely
as two bodies must occupy separate spaces but as kingdom from kingdom, starry spirit from starry spirit.

The phrases, " autonomy of the self or will," " kingdom of ends," which have been used in philosophy,
may help to make more familiar the point I am trying
to make. The phrases may not be altogether happy,
but they serve to describe the prerogative of every
human being. Each of us enjoys a limited sovereignty ;
we are persons, so unique as never to have our double,
whether in the long past history of man or in the future,
however far it may stretch. No work of art can be

compared in value with that centre which each of us calls " I," that first person, which is a cosmos richer by far than the whole vast pageant of the material universe. Something stirs in me, which is alive and new, whose every action brings novelty, generates good or evil, determines me to be more myself. No one, no finite being at any rate, can share my experiences, can endure the identical heartache and joy which are mine; nor can they bear my responsibility, commit my sins and put on the virtues I may perchance happen to have. Spirits paradoxically are at once most solitary and close in fellowship, just as they can disgrace and degrade themselves by the very fact of their possessing power over themselves as persons.

Now if there be this multiple world of beings distinct from each other, to talk of their fusion under one name is ridiculous, and still more absurd is it to call such a chimerical unity by the name of God. No one thinks of worshipping such a Noah's Ark! Whereas the God who is discerned by the mind is inaccessible by reason of his perfection. He infinitely surpasses all that the universe contains, and yet is near by virtue of his omnipotence and love which, like warm hands round a fledgling robin, keeps the heart of reality alive. We —and this is another paradox—belong most to God by maintaining the very selfhood which He has given us, and because He cannot enter into competition with us, being so exalted above us as to be incomparable, He can be the Lord and God of a world of real and not imaginary subjects. A wise and true philosophy which does justice to all the facts, which does not reduce in order to unify, reveals to us that there must be a best, if there be any things at all which are relative to some standard, and this best, this superlatively splendid and complete being, is not joined with its inferiors by some mechanical or even organic link. Being complete it gives without loss and without interference. There is nothing niggardly here; the human labourer toils to increase his own property, the human artist with alien material fashions a thing of beauty or a robot—the things are beautiful but dead; the mother from her own body gives birth to a living child, and parts from him; but God is bounty unfailing and to Him alone belongs the power and the love to bestow all, to strike not a rock but nothingness and bring forth not merely gushing water but living replicas of Himself, a spirit of beauty constituted in freedom and private ownership. From the shadow world of mere possibility He summons the varied existence we know, its roots reaching ever down to the nothingness from which it came and sustained alone by the fiat of a Will which never flags.

Is this too mad a vision, or does the thought still darken instead of enlightening the mind? Perhaps the thought moved too fast in attributing personality to the First and the Last. But surely not! There is no reason to boggle over this insertion of personality in the argument for God. Vague huge shapes, indeed, beset the imagination when it tries to picture the content of thought uplifted, and some philosophers tricked by their fancy have preferred to fall back on a sorry language about Wholes and Absolutes and impersonal or supra-personal Deity or Mind spelt with a capital. Mind belongs to a subject and such a subject is necessarily personal inasmuch as a being who thinks is bound to be aware of himself and so guardian of himself. One who is a person belongs to himself; he has some degree of self-jurisdiction. Material objects are not persons; they are intelligible but not intelligent. Once, however, the order of intelligent beings is reached, then intelligence and personality go hand in hand, and as we approach near to the burning bush of divinity, we can see that here alone is there complete selfhood, an interior life so rich as to require no supplement or assistance from without, and therefore complete personality. If from the Christian Revelation we learn besides that there is a further secret of happy giving and union within the divine life, this does not disturb our conclusions so much as flood them with light as when a mountain slope is caught by the setting sun.

So far I have been developing the statement that theism is necessary if our intellect is to be satisfied. The argument used is only a preliminary to the main contention of this book that the theistic and especially the Christian ideal is superior to all others. Before going on, however, to consider a second argument which will be put forward to show that theism alone offers a complete moral ideal, it may be well to summarize what has already been said. The mind by its very nature searches for an explanation of all it meets, and as there are so many different objects and items of experience a series of isolated explanations will not suffice ; they too must have some connection, some order. In other words, if there be truth, there must be some unity in the universe. Furthermore, this unity must be of a certain kind, one, namely, which allows for many distinct and relatively independent natural objects. If there be a kitten there must be a cat, and if there be a ship there must have been a builder, and when we cast around for a connection between the two, one solution is obvious and one is ridiculous. We must not say the unifying principle is a curious hybrid, called the kitten cat or builder ship, though some of our modern wiseacres are fond of talking like this ; as when Julian Huxley invents the word " mentoid " to cover the relation of mind and body or matter, and Lloyd Morgan faced with real novelty in nature and also, as he thinks with evolution, christens the two " emergent evolution." This is magnificent but scarcely real scientific warfare. It is more like the story of Pyramus and Thisbe as played by Quince and Bottom. The good old story-tellers were nearer the mark when they sang of the house that Jack built, for the connection is obviously one of dependence. When a horse unexpectedly wins a race, we usually find the experts tracing its pedigree back to some famous sire or mare, and as soon as that is done the tipsters and the public give a sigh of satisfaction as their mind is at rest. So too if on a desert island good Crusoe finds some tiny streams of fresh water, he will, if he be wise, search for their source. Those who deny a God are like wrecked mariners who take no heed of the source and are even prepared to deny that there need be any ; or again they resemble men who being provided with milk they know not whence proceed to kill all the cattle and the goats as of no account. Without God everything dries up. Leave Him out of our explanations and the life of thought is decapitated. Maine de Biran, that philosopher of inner experience, wrote after a period of scepticism :

Job says : *Si Deus non est, quid ergo est ?* This sublime thought is a flash of light. If God does not exist, everything is but illusion, but a lie ; the order which we perceive in nature exists only in our brain, *velut aegri somnia*. Nothing has any rational justification, there is no order, no real constancy in phenomena. Can we have recourse to hazard ? What is hazard ?

Not that really we can be in doubt that the world exists —Maine de Biran exaggerates here—but we are left with the book of nature and no explanation of how it comes to be a book and not a series of meaningless scratches.

I now turn to the second of the great constituents of any ideal, goodness. The word covers many things and I will not stop to make a dry analysis of it, hoping that as we proceed readers will recognize what they would wish to mean by it. All of us are familiar with

95

the language of " conscience," " duty " and " virtue,"
though their simple meaning has been rubbed out,
rewritten and written over countless times : unreflective
persons and peoples have had their codes, their heroes
and saints, and thinkers have in every age tried to formulate the ideal of human life and communicate the secret
of happiness. The trouble is that there is such a difference between appearances and truth, the first expectations of youth and the lessons of experience, and moreover the way of duty and of pleasure so soon divides
sharply. We suffer too from an illusion it is very
difficult to destroy. Everything that we are not seems
to us desirable, a sure fund of happiness ; the boy
chafes at the restrictions of youth and counts the time
till he will be at the top of his school and free to do
what he will, and I suppose that the girl has visions of
herself in the ball-room of the world, the cynosure of
all eyes. Yet as we approach each new experience it
becomes grey and dull, the servant only of still further
experiences, and before we know where we are our
chief claim to self-respect has become the power to
impart information and counsel, desired or not, to those
younger than ourselves.

Spartam nactus es, hanc exorna, convert the present
into gold, such is the antidote to the common illusion
of the future, and the question then arises, what kind
of golden ingot brings final peace to human ambitions.
A number of wise men tell us that the answer is contained already in what has been said. Seize the moment

and live it fully, sucking out of it, to use an old illustration, all the honey that is lingering there. Walter
Pater talked in this vein at times when he felt especially
drawn to some of the old Greek and Roman pleasure-
seekers, as he imagined them to be. If we look around
at our own friends we shall no doubt call to mind not
a few who seem to be of the same fraternity. They
may be lazy or concentrated, still or active, and they
refuse to allow themselves to be disturbed or drawn
away from the happy nook or occupation they have
chosen. Obviously such a life has many forms ; the
good man at the bar with his glass beside him or with
his feet on the mantelpiece in his shirt-sleeves before
the fire is brother to the æsthete who has surrounded
himself with *objets d'art* and even to the philanderer or
club bore. Obviously there is also a great dissimilarity
between the orgiastic delight of the sensualist, the
rapture of the poet and saint and the bank-holiday
excitement which many carry into their hours of leisure.
Both those who are in pursuit of some distant ideal
and those who refuse to bother about the future may
try to adorn their momentary dwelling-place and exhaust
the good in the present moment. Perhaps therefore
we should keep in one class only those who refuse to
be ambitious for far-off things, the folk we know so
well who take life as it comes and seem to want nothing
more. They are opposed not only to the adventurous
but also to the hedonists who deliberately maintain
that the object of life is to find as much pleasure as is

possible in the present moment. These latter do at any rate assert that there is an object in life, some ideal which befits all men.

The hedonist, whether of the extreme variety just mentioned or the generous type which is associated with the name of John Stuart Mill, need not detain us, as every serious book on morals spends a chapter in refuting them. The easy-going and unambitious usually escape the criticism of the professional moralist, but the fact that such exist does raise the question whether for certain men at least happiness is not possible without any reference to God or ultimate union with Him. We must admit, I think, that just as many can pass their days in fair comfort without exercising in any noticeable degree what is called the divine gift of intelligence, so others, whose number must be uncertain, are quite blind to the visions which the sages, the Platos and Neo-Platonists, the Spinozas behold and call upon men to realize. One answer to this difficulty is that the happiness is as much negative as positive, and by that I mean that many men derive great satisfaction from the absence of disturbing factors in their lives and by comparison with what they fear they find great pleasure in what is very insignificant when weighed by other standards. Fortunately, as we know well, life gives us unexpected thrills at every corner and turning. Our first success in a game or trial of strength or in examination gives us a joy out of all proportion to the occasion, and it is with wonder and comfort we notice how easily pleased neighbours of ours can be at quite trivial triumphs, the civil servant jubilant because a correct guess of his has promoted him into a position of authority on matters of horse-racing, the grocer because the Mayor stopped to comment on his wares, young Joe because he managed to mend the bicycle for the seventh time. The life of man is made up of these tiny joys, and the life and death experiences of a Nansen or Talbot Clifton or Mollison are reproduced in their own way in Tooting and Hambleden. *Corpus non animam mutant qui trans mare currunt.*

In addition we must remember that joys are relative to the fears and pains which precede them and are enhanced by surprise and lessened by disappointment. To Gandhi emerging from his fast the taste of food must be different from that which a don experiences at high table when eating his savoury; the rustic crossing the street by the Madeleine in Paris feels akin to the climbers of Everest; a hole in five is a romance to the tyro in golf and a vexation to Bobby Jones, and a small bounty to a workman with a wife and family which takes away that gnawing sense of insecurity makes him happier than Crœsus. We must be thankful to Providence that it has so chequered human life with light and shade and made it possible to find paradisal moments even in the worst slums. Because this is so we are able to see in part at least why so many do not seem to be roused by the pictures of an ultimate bliss which the saints and sages draw for them. It may

99

well be, however, that at moments all feel within them a longing for something over and beyond the daily round of duties and pleasures and realize that they are the actors in a drama of infinite complexity and that the whole world is hushed and expectant on their choice. Such intimations will in all likelihood be vague or disguised under concrete symbols. Just as there is truth in the remark that the Russian Communist conceals many of the motives of religion under titles which seem to deny them and pursues materialism with a spiritual passion, and just as glory and fatherland and home came to mean much the same thing to French and German and English during the Great War, so the enthusiasms of the ordinary man contain far more than his words express or his mind realizes. We see through a glass darkly and the darkness it is which makes the greatest impression on the senses. Our nature is such that the pure beauty, the radiance of eternity, has to be split up to become multicoloured before it is recognized; we must descend in order to mount up, go through dark passes of Thermopylæ to reach the shining plains, for unless the grain of wheat fall into the ground it shall not bear fruit.

It has not been sufficiently observed how necessary it is for man to turn down the lights in order to see truth properly, how, like some tiny insect, he makes a skein wherethrough to peer or sinks like the oyster into the ooze to secure tranquillity. Doughty wrote of the Semites sitting " to the eyes in a cloaca but with brows

touching heaven," and it is the lot of all of us, as the
psychologists tell us in more technical terms, to enslave
the immaterial like a djinn in a vessel and so give it a
local habitation and a name. The idler, the nurse
Simpson, the potterer in the garden, the clerk who never
fails, may not appear to be dazzled by dreams like Shelley
or Blake, but they are idealists all the same and see
infinity in the palm of the hand and eternity in an hour.
This being so, appearances are deceptive and we must
not count the cosy happy before they are dead.

Another consideration which is difficult enough to state
will help to confirm this. Religious enthusiasts are in
the habit of telling their neighbours and strangers that
this world is only an ante-room to that of eternity, a kind
of cold bath and physical exercise before breakfast. The
puzzle, if this be so, is that the majority of people are
so content to remain in it and regard death with abhor-
rence. So content, in fact, are they that they forget the
after-life altogether and talk in terms of happiness on
earth and generation after generation plots and schemes
to make a world fit for heroes to live in. There can be
no doubt that intense joy can be found in this life, and
whatever truth there be in the religious warnings this
joy demands explanation. One simple reason is no
doubt that God is not niggardly and that for human
beings endowed with reason and emotions and in process
of perfecting themselves and deciding their fate He
provides all that is requisite for them to be human and
all also that may help as an incentive to look beyond to

the supreme beauty of which earthly joys serve as distant
copies. This answer is certainly valid, but another can
also be given which, though subtle, may nevertheless
help considerably to an understanding of our condition
in this life. Composed as we are of spirit as well as
matter we cannot regard ourselves and our actions as
just means to something beyond; we leave something
complete and final behind after every choice, something
irrevocable and imperishable. Unlike the process at
Cowley where bit by bit a Morris car comes to be and
the bits have no significance save in reference to the
completed article, our growth to a better state is accomplished by the very being who is advancing and yet to
be. We are therefore in a certain sense already ourselves; we are the motor-car which has to be turned
out, and at every step we sign our names and declare
our business and take full responsibility. The philosophers have described this in saying that we are ends as
well as means, that we possess a kind of autonomy and
stamp our actions with a royal mark. If we bear the
responsibility of evil and can be arraigned for crime long
since committed, and if in our free choices we can so commit ourselves that our choice is a final one to be judged
as a mortal offence fit for everlasting punishment or so
pleasing in its love as to deserve an immortal reward,
it follows that in the very journey of the soul to perfection it can " expand the present," " lift the present itself
above its time fetters and convey a sense of the eternal."
Hence it is that in all adventures, whether it be of the

first thrust of love, the discovery by a Newton or Pasteur, the beating of a speed record in the air, or the sight of new lands off the Spanish Main, just as much as in the momentous decisions in a life at home, the soul holds for a brief time life in its entirety and in recollection sees that it was good.

If the reader has followed this explanation he will be in the position, I hope, to appreciate why so many remain content with their life on this earth and pay so little attention to those who summon them to prepare for what is to come after death. They all obey Aristotle and " play the immortal as far as possible," and their very readiness to do so is evidence for the Christian teaching. Where they go wrong is in blinding themselves to the fact that their supposed happiness is shot through with the colours of decay and death. Though our acts are imperishable we pass on, and though the old comfort themselves with the memories of past experiences which they try to live again, age in time robs them even of this pleasure. At the best, as Virginia Woolf has written :

Life had been imperfect, an unfinished phrase. It had been impossible for me, taking snuff as I do from any bagman met in a train, to keep coherency—that sense of the generations, of women carrying pitchers to the Nile, of the nightingale who sings among conquests and migrations.

The seasons pass and we with them, and the expectations, so bright in youth, whether for the self or for the race, remain unfulfilled. Actions which cost us an agony in their decision and bore on their face a cosmic significance seem now to be borne out further and further into the sea like a log caught by a receding tide. *Ou sont les neiges d'antan?* Leonidas is dead and the pass of Thermopylæ a resort for tourists. Yet the harvest is assured, and if our hopes have received partial frustration they will be satisfied at an hour we know not and in a place we have not yet visited. The error, as we have noticed so often before, is to mistake the twilight for the dawn, and then to delude the simple with hopes which can never be verified in this life. The author of the *Gold Falcon* tells us that his hero, Manfred, when

gliding and turning with the others over the ice, learned once again that the true spirit of man is not that which longs for immortality or resurrection through another as saviour, but the spirit that in the joy of effortless play holds the body invisible and suspended as the sun—the inner sun which strives to shine out of every man towards the great sun in heaven.

We could not have a better example of the state of mind I have been attempting to describe which catches eternity in a moment, and of the fallacy of identifying it with that completeness which is necessary for genuine and unfailing happiness.

As an escape from this conclusion there are many nowadays who would say that the old creed of the greatest happiness of the greatest number is good enough for them, and there is a minority which frankly teaches self-indulgence and the joys of sensualism. Neither is very consistent, and if I were asked to give the name of one who was a pure sensualist or pure altruist, it would be difficult to give an answer. D. H. Lawrence has shocked many by his gospel of the flesh, but his admirers have this of truth in their defence of him, that he was inspired by a faith which decried beastliness as much as it warred against the hypocrisy of the intellectuals. Others contented themselves with violent abuse of the Puritans and Grundies; Lawrence saw further and accused his generation of a denial of life, of taking it at second hand, of possessing paper souls and making themselves eunuchs for the sake of no kingdom of God. If he exaggerated and if his message be far less original than he thought, this need not be a matter of surprise in an age of Bernard Shaws and Christian Science. The others one might name do indeed confuse the reins with the heart, but if, like Mr. Richard Aldington, they proclaim the glory of bodily experiences and are sure that any other gospel is spiritual lechery, they are so unhappy and embittered in their tone that they can hardly expect others to emulate their experience.

The more generous form of hedonism is that which seeks for the greatest happiness of the greatest number, and to their honour many of the disciples of this creed have worked unsparingly for the betterment of social conditions and the emancipation of the working classes. But so topsy-turvy is our world that we have the spectacle of a large number of human beings, in the East as in the West, adopting that very poverty we are so anxious to remove as the quickest road to happiness. Of course, there is no comparison between voluntary and enforced poverty ; nevertheless, the paradox does bring out an essential defect in the doctrine of the greatest happiness. Its advocates seem to have confused conditions for happiness with happiness itself, and this confusion shows itself in a problem which is very much before us at the present day. That problem is contained in the question, what are we to do with our leisure ? The rapid advance of applied science conjures up a time when man will have little to do. Will he then be more happy ? If we are to judge by the evidence of civil servants and officers of the army and navy, by the conduct of those who frequent the clubs, the answer is in the negative. The present is almost always banal as compared with the picture of the future, and we compare one with the other as duties with freedom, labour with rest. Thus it comes about that freedom takes on the appearance of something positive and we make it an end in itself. Bitter is the disappointment and shallow is the philosophy which thinks its task is accomplished when it has laid the way clear for liberty. Let us by all means get rid of our shackles, but we must not confuse them with props or rods of discipline.

The advocate of the greatest happiness for the greatest number must, therefore, tell us very clearly what kind of happiness he has in mind. Many times we have been told that this is pleasure, and we wait on those who will

explain to us how pleasure of itself can be an end at all
and show how duty and virtue can be made its servants.
From time immemorial this theory of pleasure has been
raked fore and aft by serious thinkers. It would be
waste of time to reproduce their arguments and besides
we are only concerned with its attractiveness as an ideal.
As such it seems to contain elements which belong to
the ideal which is in the heart of man, but of itself it is
insufficient and it fails to provide what it promises. The
same may be said of Stoicism. Whether it be the pleasure
of isolated moments of pure joy or comfort or the giving
of pleasure to others, it does not cover all we want nor
does it take sufficient account of moral goodness. The
Cinema and the B.B.C. provide universal pleasure or try
to do so, and they would be the first to admit that they
are forced to compromise ; they have to allow subjects
which they themselves do not wholly approve ; they have
to offend one section of the community in order to give
pleasure to another, and—what is most important of
all—they control their efforts to please by rules or
standards which have nothing to do with pleasure. If
pleasure be so controlled it cannot itself be described as
the perfect life. And I may add that if it be not so controlled it will soon cease even to be a pleasurable one.
Pleasure without stint surfeits the palate ; it increases a
craving which becomes more and more difficult to
satisfy and it makes us less and less capable of self-
restraint. This latter effect is one of the reasons why
Kant would not admit pleasure into the realm of morality,

why too the Stoic sought to make for himself an inner chamber of the soul which should be secure against all the world's alarums and irritations.

Something of the defects in all such ideals we have already seen. In truth they fail in somewhat the same way that philosophies fail which leave out God. If we consider the condition of mankind, we see that it is one of growth and conflict; we are egged on by conscience to observe certain ideal standards and we are chastised by the scorpions of our own conscience when we yield to temptation; the spirit is willing, but the flesh is weak; what is high is approved, but it is the low to which we incline, and all men's struggles are appraised according as they attain a mastery over themselves and act heroically and unselfishly. There is something, therefore, we ought to be, some ideal to which we by nature tend. But more than this; we are not enlisted only in a campaign of self-perfection; both our duty and our love demand that we should concern ourselves with others, and our endeavour must be to make justice and love triumph at home and in city and State and wherever man has pitched his camp. Now how can we satisfy this thirst for justice and this need for self-perfection? Injustice thrives all around us. Material conditions prevent millions from expanding in this life into the full glory of their personality. Merit goes unrewarded and no one knows of the countless tiny acts of self-denial, of honesty and forgiveness which make up, thank God, the ordinary coinage of exchange between man and man.

At times the sacrifice demanded of us is bound to inter-
fere with the development of our own talents and may
even impair them, as when a mother watches over for
days and nights the sick bed of her child or a Damien
tends his lepers. Beautiful and undeniable as is the
saying of Christ that " no man hath greater love than
this, to give his life for a friend," it offers a problem for
those who deny an after-life and a God who rewards.
Do not misunderstand me. I do not say that the self-
sacrifice should be made in the hope of a reward. The
problem concerns us who see a world in which if there
be no God, the good suffer injustice, the wicked prosper
and the greatest act a man can perform, to give his life
for a friend, is in fact tragic. He dies and sees no fruit
of his sacrifice ; he gives all that he has and nature pays
no attention.

And this tragic waste comes near to each one of us
when we look in on our own state of soul. No sooner
do we come to the use of reason than we hitch our
waggon to a star ; we make for ourselves pictures of
what we shall and must be, and as the years pass the
crude first sketch transforms itself into the ideal of virtue
and grandeur of soul. The prosecution of this is thwarted
by circumstances, by health, by counter-attractions without and within. We never attain it, though—and this
is the justification of our life in this world—we live it
partially in the very acts which help us onwards to it ;
but usually our efforts are so half-hearted, so spasmodic,
so chequered with mean motives, our falls are so heavy,

that our days in retrospect look like débris. Besides, we soon realize that the horizons we thought near when we were young withdraw and open out new beauties. We never exhaust the possibilities of goodness; we come instead to recognize the unfailing limitations of our own standards. And because this is so, and indeed for many other reasons, it should become plain to us that the life of the spirit as seen in its moral activities is quite different from that of the body. The latter in a few years reaches its zenith and then begins to decline. Hardly have we reached manhood than we find that our limbs have grown too stiff to win prizes, to catch Atalantas, to box or row with the best. Let us then face without regrets the seven ages of bodily man, provided that we recognize that the spirit of man shows no such curve, that wisdom increases with the years and that moral perfection beckons to us careless of the years we may have run. But even at the moment we recognize this truth we become aware of the silence and appearance of decrepitude which the body, as it fails, may produce in the soul. Nothing is sadder than to see the unavailing struggle of the valiant will and noble mind to combat the weakness of old age. The existence of this combat is sufficient of itself to prove the discrepancy between the life of the body and the life of the spirit, and it would be tragic if indeed it meant the final collapse of the latter. Fortunately such an end is not conceivable however much certain philosophers assure us it is so. At any rate, the very contrast makes clear the vital need of an ideal which announces God as the everlasting good of man at the top of the page.

From another angle we can enforce the same conclusion. Our own efforts to reach to the complete life never succeed. Both the weakness of our will and the rapid decline of our powers are as dragons in the path. Nevertheless, the command is written in our soul and we become only miserably unhappy if we pay no attention to the moral law of our nature. Here is a dilemma we cannot escape. What we ought to be and do pricks our conscience; and the ascent, as cold as that of the Himalayas, leads to that region, where, as Plato saw, the absolute and unchanging norms of perfection dwell. Such high, pure forms freeze the very impulse they provoke, and yet we cannot ignore them. Is this not evidence that our moral philosophy and our moral life cannot be satisfied until the abstractions of goodness pass into the will and love of a Person, the will of One which "must be done on earth as it is in heaven"? Duty and interest are for us so often apart and morality is thought to be too austere to include affection. But if goodness be only a dim word concealing a Person who is most lovable, and if duty be only the echo of a voice calling us to union with Himself, then indeed our philosophy can take life and we be carried by force of that love into a perfection and happiness which cannot be surpassed. A final end which is impersonal does not make us take wing, whereas the thought of One for whom we were made, who can respond to our approaches and our appeals, and who can love us more than we love ourselves touches both our heart and our mind and fires us to admiration and affection. Nothing which is below ourselves can become a worthy ideal, and if we say that the Absolute, or whatever we please to call it, is so vast and immense as to be supra-personal, then we are in danger of fobbing ourselves off with a featureless concept, which is in actual content less than ourselves. The living God, on the other hand, by His majesty fills us with reverence, by His sovereignty awakens our fidelity and by His love makes us to long after Him, if happily we may find Him and enjoy union with Him.

I have said that the human spirit is essentially solitary, that possessing ourselves no one else can possess us and experience just what we suffer and enjoy. And yet the dream ever hovers before our minds of a union such that I understand even as I am understood; " two distincts, division none ; number there in love was slain." The dream is an empty one if we hope for such a union with a fellow-creature and for the reason that whatsoever can stand in comparison with us or make together with us two things can never overlap so as to be two in one. But with God all things are possible. He does not enter into comparison with us and we cannot make an addition sum of God and ourselves, no more than a small a can enlarge the capital A. To say, for instance, that God and the world is larger or greater than God by Himself has no meaning ; it is like measuring a stone and the thought of it or eternity with an hour. The divine power and love which are all things already superabundantly are like sunlight travelling over a hillside ; they reveal ; they do not jar or collide with what is there. Examples fail here because they must always be of finite objects which are necessarily spiky and exclusive. I said that we can judge the worth in the scale of existences by their power to break down their own barriers and become worldwide in their interests, and that this gift went paradoxically with their increasing self-possession. God is not shut off at all ; He is in no sense a prisoner, having no limitations. Nothing escapes Him, and if He remains Himself it is by perfection and not by any subtraction, not by any provincialism or nationalism, not by any dog-in-the-manger exclusiveness. God, moreover, as our creator has entrance into His creation and knows it intimately as His. If then out of His condescension He extends His love to man and gives Himself as our end and bliss, we have more than was contained in our dream. The whole of our life is orientated to an end ; our scattered forces are focused together ; our aim becomes definite, and instead of suffering from the disease of self-love, of putting ourselves, our happiness or even virtue, in the first place, we are drawn out of ourselves by an ideal which transcends and elevates us. A sickly and degenerate generation is sceptical of everything save its own needs ; it cannot keep its eyes off itself, and it is for ever talking of experience and peering into and poking about in the subterranean chambers of the soul. A full-blooded race cares for none of these things; it is up with the sun, intent on its occupation, takes stock of things all round, is responsive to external sights and voices, to novelty and the myriad invitations of beauty, and has belief and loyalties.

Theism, therefore, is the fourth note which makes a star, for not only can no clear aim in life be discerned, no end to direct our conduct, without God, but, as I have said, we are left with a topsy-turvy world in which injustice often triumphs, eternal values are spilt and apparently lost and in this waste thousands of millions of men pass without record to an untimely death. More concretely still, there is no temporal ideal which is safe against mischance, there is no certain alliance between duty and happiness or enlightened self-interest, no final meeting-place in this life of self-perfection and self-sacrifice. If man continues to throw away everything, even life itself, for the sake of others, he does so because ineradicably in his breast he is sure that the sacrifice cannot be in vain. This in itself is an argument for immortality, for the existence of a God who will bring all things to a happy conclusion, but in a stark universe bereft of God such heroism is little else than tragedy, a noble folly which brings with it irreparable loss.

Both truth, then, and goodness lose their fair colour if God be taken away from the ideal of man. And the third in the trilogy of values, beauty, also suffers diminution. Much has been written on this the most elusive of all the three, and I may be excused if I say little about it. There are some who say that it is nothing more than a compound of the other two, and indeed it is hard to separate it off from them, so intertwined is it with truth and goodness. To the Greeks it was, perhaps, the fairest name of all, and Plato, when his talk, like an aeroplane, took off from the ground, circled round this star of beauty, and even Aristotle, when he wished to describe a type of friendship higher than that of utility and pleasure, almost invariably called it the fair and beautiful. There is a sentence of St. Augustine which, for some of us, is the most haunting in all literature, and it runs: *Sero Te amavi, Pulchritudo tam antiqua et tam nova*, "Too late have I loved Thee, Beauty ever ancient and ever fresh." Augustine and so many others seem to have gathered up in the word "beauty" all the desires of their heart and to have tried in this one word to express the inexpressible. Beauty has this about it, that it appears to set off the object or person we behold in the most fitting garb, to bring out all that is best there and in such a way as to appeal most strongly to the beholder. If you like it can be called the outside of the cup, the radiant look, the festal air. We speak of a scene or friend looking its or her best, and from the earliest ages of the life of man upon this earth there have been moments and moods when by dress and dance and music mankind has obeyed the call to make a feast of beauty. The display and pageantry are not motived by vanity; they mark a communal act of man. I say communal because beauty may be prepared in solitude, but like the

Betrothed in Rossetti's picture it comes forth as a bride to enchant the eyes of all beholders.

This then is one if not the chief of the characteristics of beauty, that it is worth made manifest, Ulysses with the grace given by a goddess upon his features, an Aphrodite risen from the waves. And if we consult philosophy we shall receive confirmation of this, for it would seem that nature after much travailing comes at a timeless moment known to itself to birth, and as the buds open and youth reaches its efflorescence beauty descends upon them. What is latent is drawn out by secret law or by self-expression, and voluntarily or involuntarily this expression is a public proclamation, a device to call the attention of all to nature at its best. But alas! its effort is soon exhausted; the ecstasy of perfect life is soon over, and there is " no waving off of these most mournful messengers . . . of grey," " there is nothing can be done to keep at bay age and age's evils, hoar hair, ruck and wrinkle, drooping, dying, death's worst, winding sheets, tombs and worms and tumbling to decay." Beauty shares the fate of all mortal children, and we who would build our tabernacle to watch it for eternity have to descend the hillside heavy with a sense of loss.

But before counting our losses and seeing whether once again theism heaps up a treasure which is not consumed, let us follow out, a little further, one or two distinctions which are commonly made, such as that between natural and æsthetic or artistic beauty. So far we have been writing of natural beauty, and perhaps concentrating too much on a certain type. There are many questions here which we must leave alone after having stated the answer to them which seems right. Nature appeals to us through the senses, by sight and sound and smell, and there are some who would have us believe that beauty is located only in the sensible world and that it is in the senses that the enjoyment consists. Probably, therefore, they would say, it is relative to us. Such a view is short-sighted. Our pleasure is not due merely to the senses being tickled. Animals most likely have a similar experience, but they do not pause in contemplation; they are not aware of something which is more than ourselves, of something timeless and absolute. Moreover, we clearly distinguish between the titivation of our sense which for example we may experience in touch and taste and the more exalted joy we feel when we suddenly hear a skylark or some boy singing. In seeing we are hardly aware at all that it is a sensation; it is so close to thought that we use the word perception indifferently for beholding an object with the eye and with the mind, and besides part at least of our pleasure is due to associations and to patterns, which are complex and harmonious and unified.

The truth is, I would maintain, that as a rule we combine with sense an intellectual satisfaction. No doubt a flash of light, a splash of colour, a border, for instance, of blue viscaria and yellow and red eschscholtzia, can delight the eye as honey pleases the palate, though

even in these cases the effect can scarcely be compared
with that of a red rag to a bull or the fakir's piping on a
cobra.   We cannot do justice to our reactions to beauty
unless we admit that the spirit too takes part in the
discovery.   Now the complete joy of the spirit is in
truth, and truth consists in that intuition into the essence
of ourselves and what is different from ourselves.   This
perfect insight is never given to us in this life ; our fate
is to work by the sweat of our face and to reach conclusions laboriously.   Sometimes the mathematician dealing
with abstractions has, we are told, an experience like to
that of æsthetic pleasure, and if this is so it will bear out
what I am trying to argue.   Constituted as we are of
sense and intellect, and meeting reality only through the
senses, an ideal intellectual intuition or insight is forbidden us ; we see the exteriors of things, we can know
their activities and so by scientific methods we can
arrive at some knowledge of what those things are.   If,
as the mathematician does, we separate off a certain aspect
of the real—call it the numerable or measurable or what
you like—then possibly in that confined area something
resembling intuition may be enjoyed.   But we can do
better than that ; we can soothe ourselves with an
experience of a lower order which is a mimesis or imitation of intellectual intuition.   That is to say, we can
enjoy the intuition of the senses.   The sensible world
is the real as it appears to us ; the senses bring it to us
and that is their function.   But since they do it directly
and manifest to us, as it were, nature's bloom, they bring

also that joy to the spirit which we call æsthetic pleasure. We rest from the striving, the toil and labour of living and learning, and forget all in the pleasure of æsthetic contemplation, thereby giving ourselves a foretaste of an ideal condition of joy, in which truth and beauty would blend in one happy vision. It is for this reason that we do not learn directly from beauty ; we stop for a moment to anticipate and to refresh ourselves, and those who sacrifice truth and goodness for the sake of it remain in an antechamber of the temple where as we hope all three shall be as one.

If this be so, we have an explanation of the pleasure which is peculiar to art. Its object is something different from that of all our other activities. They are concerned with the real world, where our experiences are fortunate or unfortunate, good and pleasant, or evil and disastrous. We are checked by real sorrow and pain, and every step we take means that we must either walk straightforward or crookedly. In art, on the other hand, we, so to say, suspend the actual world and all that is practical in it. We do not rise up to stop Othello murdering Desdemona or warn Œdipus that he is loading the dice against himself. We enjoy the dramatic irony, and in concerts or when reading poetry we ignore the false theology of the Ring and the atheism of Shelley. The actual ought not to intrude, and that is one reason why it is easier to enjoy the work of a Lucretius than *The Dynasts* of Hardy, the pessimism latent in Omar Khayyám than *The Shropshire Lad*. No one could be so insensitive as to dramatize a friend's bereavement, and if poetry is on occasions written on the death of friends an *In Memoriam* has for object to remove the atmosphere of the death chamber and take us into an immortal region. Art then is at one remove from life. We are no longer conscripts moving down the trenches. The anxieties, the calculations, the instinct of self-preservation, these disappear; we are transported into a world of make-belief, of beauty without responsibility. And if this be so, is it not an intimation of a state which is paradisal, where even evil has had its sting removed?

Note.—Hardly had I written these last lines when I came across a passage in Mr. Whitehead's latest book, *Adventures of Ideas*, and as it seems to have been made to supplement them, I quote it:

As soon as high consciousness is reached, the enjoyment of existence is entwined with pain, frustration, loss, tragedy. Amid the passing of so much beauty, so much heroism, so much daring, Peace is then the intuition of permanence. It keeps vivid the sensitiveness to the tragedy, and it sees the tragedy as a living agent persuading the world to aim at fineness beyond the faded level of surrounding fact. Each tragedy is the disclosure of an ideal—What might have been, and was not: What can be. The tragedy was not in vain. This survival power in motive force, by reason of appeal to reserves of Beauty, marks the difference between the tragic evil and the gross evil. The inner feeling belonging to this grasp of the service of tragedy is Peace—the purification of the emotions.

We have hardly done more than glance at this fascinating subject of beauty, but if the impression be fair, certain conclusions follow at once. In the ideal state beauty will for ever refresh our souls. As Whitehead says, peace is the intuition of permanence and the purification of the passions which is given in art discloses to us a region where we shall no longer be torn with doubt or troubled by anxiety, where love beholding face to face that which it had so long desired will rush to its perfection and be made one with the object which calls its name. Such peace within, such permanence of joy and fruition, what are they but the epithalamium of beauty ? Beauty is so far relative that it varies to some extent with our sensitive apparatus ; too strong a light hurts the eye and to ears differently habituated musical intervals have a more and less pleasant sound But though we must admit this dose of relativity in our appreciation of beauty we have already shown that the sensitive organism is not sufficient to explain our delight in what is beautiful in nature and in art. In the latter we make to ourselves graven images of an invisible and spiritual beauty—not for worship but for joy—and just because the spiritual world " yonder " is dim and pursued with effort and by the abstractions of the intellect we love to come near to it in our imagination and to embody it in all manner of sensible forms. There in sensible experience we approach to intuition and to ecstasy and are as carefree as those who take holiday in dance and song after labouring in the sun for their livelihood. We may even by the indulgence of providence find this joy in our very work, if that work be our own and if the labour of it be to the making of objects of natural use as the fisherman makes and mends his nets and the woodsman slices his wood and sharpens it for his craft. In such toil the labourer has ever before his mind the end his instrument would serve, but woe betide the artist who separates beauty from truth and goodness, who makes an idol of his art and calls out that beauty is the end of life. He has betrayed his calling and he has made a sacrament of the shadow instead of the substance. To what serves mortal beauty? If we accept it gratefully and keep it ever in the train of its two sisters goodness and truth, we shall learn the answer to the question. But if like so many who would escape the inexorable laws of life we substitute art and its delectations for duty and sacrifice, we shall lose beauty in the end and see our Valhalla disappear in flames. The poet and the musician know that their vocation is beset with perils, that over-indulgence in their art does not feed the soul and that in this life men cannot live by beauty alone. The struggle for existence of which the scientists speak belongs supremely to man's lot, but whereas with sensitive beings joy seems to be given in the very act of living, with man, torn by two worlds, the joy vouchsafed comes from achievement, from the constant premonition in beauty of a final happiness. Man is torn and divided; he has no lasting stay; he is whipped by his conscience ever forward; he is too mighty to be at home in this world; too tumultuous to be at rest. His ecstasy is not therefore in the act of living; he is happiest at the moment of dying to himself, and the music in his soul begins when he sets the rhythms of this world, of his body and his senses to an immortal theme.

Beauty therefore gleams athwart the life of man and is his protection, accompanying him as the angel led the young Tobias without revealing his name. It is not meant to be taken as an ideal which enfranchises us from common work, from the precepts of morality or from religion. It cannot take their place, as it is either an illumination accompanying their presence or it is conditioned by them and withers when they are neglected. Truth and goodness we have seen shine out in their full splendour only when the shadowy face of the earth is lit up by the presence of God, but beauty, like a tiny Pan which has escaped out of control, is for ever beckoning us to take our ease or search for our pleasure without thought of trial or future or the unsteadiness of our appetites. All then is forgotten or put on one side with an impatient gesture. Experience for the moment is worth whatever may come, and the immediate thrill of that experience may be so great that all else for the moment seems trivial or like the muttering of dull and anæmic conventionalists. But the aftermath is always the same.

The hoots of the far-off engines in the night, the sudden noise of the rain had an accent I had never heard before but which was unmistakable to me; on other occasions they never spoke like that—rather, on other occasions my ears were not attuned to their truth-speaking voices. They told me that in fact we lived in a cardboard box, maudlin, shoddy and in those parts where it might once have been expressive of some inner substance, long superannuated, and that all our activities, science, religion, philosophy, society, money-making were no more than efforts to keep this truth suppressed. They told me that I lived in a void, that there were chasms about me and at my feet into which the moment my desires ceased, I should disappear. For all is vanity and illusion, as the Preacher said, and flies to dust the moment our desires, perpetually springing, cease to sustain it.[1]

Thus the heresy burns itself out as the stick which had served for the rocket of fire falls after the illumination in some obscure place.

[1] *Jack Robinson*, by George Beaton, pp. 269–70.

CHAPTER III

THE IDEA OF GOD: THE MINIMUM

I PROPOSE in this chapter to look at religion and theology from an outsider's standpoint, in order to be able to discuss coolly and in the society of the inquirers and sceptically minded what must be admitted about God by any human being. For this reason I have added the word, "minimum," to the title of this chapter. By acting thus I hope to escape from the embarrassing situation in which writers on God usually find themselves. If they write soberly and try to prove their case they are accused by the votaries of religion of having betrayed their cause, of having written about God as if He were a theorem. On the other hand, if they write religiously as those who have tasted of the fountain of living waters, they are told by the scientists and philosophers that they are begging the question or relying on some personal experience which is not shared by all. By reserving the best wine to the last and beginning with a thin wine, almost as tasteless as cold water, I hope to be able to convince the well-disposed inquirer that any thinking man is bound to accept the existence of a divine being. Having thus argued with him in the outer courts of the temple I can then take him within that he may worship.

Belief in God is common amongst simple people. It is taken for granted as belief in a world around them filled with streams and stars and living things and human beings. Doubt belongs to sophisticated ages. That, of course, does not prove anything one way or the other, but it does suggest a method of procedure, a rough analysis first of what is believed and following on that the examination of it. This is the method adopted by most men with regard to their beliefs. From childhood onward they are taught by word and by reading about persons present and past, about places and events, of things visible and invisible, and with the implicit faith of the young they believe most of what they are told. Then they hear criticism and they begin themselves to test their beliefs, and nowadays one of the first to have to undergo examination is God. There are some teachers of religion who resent this inquiry, or at any rate they dispose of it by denying that the subject of religion is open to reason. They retort by asking whether good judgment in music can be proved by logic, whether the moral intuitions of a delicate conscience can be reduced to casuistry. Now to many this may sound a good answer. After all, this cloak of rationalism put on by the young or old sceptic makes him look ridiculous; he neither does nor can apply his reason to all his knowledge. He parades it when

he wants to be rid of some belief or to embarrass
another and score off him. How many, for instance,
could prove their own existence? And as to the
evidence to the existence of others the high philosophers
are still wrangling about the nature of the argument.
A defence like this is probably of great use to shake
the confidence of the rationalist, to show him that he
does not carry all the cards. Nevertheless, it does not
seem to me to be altogether satisfactory and it has
pleased very few of the admittedly great philosophers.
It does not go to the heart of the matter, and it does not
save the belief always of those who are honestly in doubt.
The man who hears an argument against God and feels
its efficacy ought to have that argument answered, and
the best answer is to show him reasons which cannot
be rebutted. The retort given above, as it stands, is
negative. It says that religion is like æsthetics or moral
intuition ; but this may well be questioned, as it is a
mere assertion. Æsthetics is concerned primarily with
sensible beauty, and quite clearly what gives joy to
the senses is not wholly an affair of reason. Again, moral
intuition must mean either the grasp of very simple
and fundamental principles in morality or a combination
of good judgment with sound instincts. Neither is
parallel with religious experience and knowledge. A
few examples suffice to make a child realize that cruelty
is not a virtue and when we have to come to a moral
decision in difficult and delicate cases we are considering what particular action should be done. Perhaps,

however, those who talk of moral experience in this connection have in mind that vivid realization of duty or perfection which is often recounted in the histories of good men. Here undoubtedly there is a judgment of the relative worth of objects and ideals which is not out of place when we come to think of the nature of God and His works.

But for the moment we are not considering the nature of God. We are in the position of a man who is accused of talking poetry instead of sense; we are called upon to produce our hero or at least certain evidence for his existence. Of course, we cannot think of God without attributing some recognizable character to Him. This our adversary will admit since his whole contention is that what people call God is nothing more than a fictitious entity. We maintain, on the contrary, that we can argue from facts which atheist and believer alike accept to the existence of a unique being, which ought rightly to be called God since it is He who corresponds with what all religious persons and all theistic philosophies, the vast majority of mankind, in fact, have had in mind in however confused a way. What is this idea running through all religions? A few years ago it would have been thought very wrong to give a simple and categorical answer. Religion was in the melting-pot, and various apothecaries made new prescriptions; we were told much about totemism and animism of fear and magic and superstition, and the gallant Andrew Lang took down the jawbone of an

ass and hit many heads with it. Now that the fight
has calmed down the anthropologist is content to admit
an element even in primitive religions which is the same
in germ as that which gives value to its highest forms,
and so for the sake of argument we will take this tiny
concession as enough. On the inner side this element
can be described in terms of reverence or awe, the
emotional and spiritual attitude which is expressed in
adoration and worship; on the outer side the object
inciting and inspiring this reaction is the numinous or
the divine or the holy. It is in these terms that a growing number of authorities speak. Let us see, therefore,
what we can do with them.

We are told that mankind has constantly believed in
a being, impersonal or personal, which has stirred in
the mind and heart the response of worship. If an
analysis and criticism of this statement were required,
it would have to run along the following lines. Is the
content of this belief a unique and simple idea or can
it be shown to be a compound of other ideas? Again
do we arrive at it by inference or by direct apprehension
and experience, and if it be by the latter process, then
is the numinous a character without a subject or belonging to one subject or again to many? All these questions cry for an answer, and fortunately we have an
answer to some of them, though it is not that provided
by the eminent thinkers who write about the numinous.
They are silent or make ambiguous replies, and it is
the *vox populi* which is plain and forthright. " The

earth is the Lord's and the fullness thereof." The
tribes and peoples of the world pray to a God who is
the master of life and death, the Lord of heaven and
earth, the author and end of all things; and it is this
notion of a supreme being, of infinite majesty and power,
who is indeed holy and mysterious and without defect,
which reflective reason has to justify. This is the substance of the idea of God, and the question we have
now to answer is whether some such being does in
fact exist.

We can start the argument either from nature or
ourselves. For the ordinary intelligence the argument
from nature is very simple, so simple, indeed, that
those of us with a little learning suspect a trick somewhere and would like to reject it as a nursery game.
The things we meet with in our everyday experience
had a beginning; they don't just come and go like the
smile of the Cheshire cat. Not even the youngest
child is satisfied that things are as they seem when the
conjurer produces ribbons and rabbits apparently out
of nothing. Everything that had a beginning came
from something else, and think as much as we like or
imagine, as we may, the most marvellous Ariels or
angels, all of them except one must have come from
somewhere or someone. I say except one, the superlative whom we quite naturally think of as never having
begun, as having been there all the time, the author
and maker of the world, its unknown parts just as much
as its known contents. Plenty of things happen in this

world, and no one, be he child or octogenarian, is
satisfied with the bare statement, " It happened." We
cannot help asking how and why it happened, and this
question with its answer has been drawn out in a famous
argument put in three ways. First, the happening must
have been started by someone who himself never had
to start, as he always was, is and will be ; secondly,
the happenings are what they are and related to their
antecedents not in any haphazard way. We cannot
give what we have not got, and so the kinds of things
which we come across must have been made to be
what they are by some thing or person who has the
resources to produce them. A bucket cannot be filled
with water from a well which is dry, a body be sustained
by food which has no vitamines in it, a boy be taught
history by one who knows no history. No doubt this
second form of the argument seems to have a catch in
it, and to realize its cogency the third form should be
brought into action. Examples may rise to the mind
which do not appear to fit in with it. A draught may
cause a cold and tiny causes have mighty effects. True,
but this is because we do not usually consider the total
cause ; we are merely looking for the match which set
the house on fire, and this is to return to the first argument which was concerned with the cause of the movement of something with a nature which we have taken
for granted. A game of football starts with a kick-off,
and if, as sometimes happens, the mayor or member of
Parliament has performed that task, the game can go

on quite well without him. The builders of the Pyramids are long dead and the Pyramids still stand. Such agents or causes are responsible only for the changes or developments in an object or nature which is in itself independent of them. My second argument, however, goes deeper and further, and says that what is borrowed from a source cannot be richer than the source, that the needy when they are filled must necessarily be helped by those who are richer than themselves, that we are forced to posit a cause of the multitudinous effects and events, which come and go like gleams of flickering and uncertain light, in some first cause which is beholden to nothing, because it is complete and self-sufficient. The candelabra of nature must be lighted from some unfailing source of light.

The third form of the argument is the most sure of all, though perhaps less easy. If we look at what seems most firm and self-supporting in nature and ask ourselves is it imperishable, made, shall we say ? of such granite that under no conditions whatever could we conceive it ceasing to be, we shall be bound to answer in the negative. Everything that we know has its appointed season, it endures for a while and then passes away. Ruskin in one of his poetical moods wrote of "trees for the builder's yard, flowers for the bride's chamber, corn for the granary, moss for the grave," and of the mountains which look to enjoy perpetuity:

They which at first seemed strengthened beyond the dread of any violence or change are yet also ordained to bear upon them the symbol of a perpetual fear; the tremor which fades from the soft lake and gliding river is sealed to all eternity upon the rock; and while things that pass visibly from birth to death may sometimes forget their feebleness, the mountains are made to possess a perpetual memorial of their infancy, that infancy which the prophet saw in his vision, "I beheld the earth, and lo! it was without form and void, and the heavens, and they had no light. I beheld the mountains and lo! they trembled and all the hills moved lightly."

The poetical exaggeration of this passage should not hide from us the truth contained in it. All is relative and changing; even the hardest of materials and the most substantial of forms have written in them, so to speak, a *memento mori*; they confess their indigence and frailty and have their nature and existence by permission. I almost hope that some reader will say that this is misrepresentation and at this point twist the argument away from "medieval talk of natures and forms" and make it modern by reference to atoms or ultimate particles. These then, it will be claimed, do not perish; they are the stuff of which all is made and there is no reason to suppose that they have not persisted from infinite time or everlastingly. I might reply by quoting Sir James Jeans or again Sir Arthur Eddington:

There is no doubt [as the latter says] that the scheme of physics as it has stood for the last three-quarters of a century postulates a date at which either the entities of the universe were created in a state of high organization, or pre-existing entities were endowed with that organization which they have been squandering ever since, [and again :] whoever wishes for a universe which can continue indefinitely must lead a crusade against the second law of thermodynamics.

133

Such replies, however, while they should suffice to those who appeal to the scientific Cæsar, are really a luxury or work of supererogation. Let us yield to the fancy that the world is composed of some primary elements, call them atoms or what you will—leaving out too all the complicating notions of mass energy, entropy and so forth; let us grant that these primary elements have persisted from infinite time and may continue to do so. Have we by such admissions damaged our argument? In the terms in which I first stated it, yes; but that is because, for the sake of simplicity, I took the word perishable as equivalent to the actual passing away of things. Both observation and science, physical and historical, bear witness to this passing away, but in fact the argument would hold even supposing that some material elements were spared this fate. By "perishable" I mean not so much that things do fade away as that there is no intrinsic reason why they should not do so. Before a Ming vase we are aware of its beauty and at the same time of the need of guarding it carefully lest it break. In the same way the entities of which the scientists speak, be they real or fictitious, are divisible at least in thought. They do not certify their own necessary existence, as is shown by the fact that we cannot be absolutely certain that they may not be replaced by still more ultimate particles, and we can conceive of their vanishing away or having no place in other possible worlds. They cannot be a satisfactory explanation of everything since they do not even explain themselves, their being in existence at all. We cannot write *finis* to our philosophical search when we have found them, any more than we could be satisfied if on looking out of our window we saw a fair with merry-go-rounds continually in motion; and even if this fair went on indefinitely and our friends told us that its beginning was unknown and that for all they knew it would never cease, we should still be bound to have many questions to ask. The merry-go-rounds could not be in motion or what they are without something else or some other being also existing. By their very nature they are dependent.

In enlarging on this question of the ultimate source of the material world I have been attempting to make clear that our mind requires not only a supreme and ultimate being who is responsible for there being any happenings at all, who must too have had all the requisites to produce the positive reality we know—for something cannot arise out of nothing—but a being as well who is to our conditioned, relative, fugitive world as the unconditioned, the absolute and the self-subsistent. There is nothing we know of in the universe of which we can say, " Behold! what is," applying to it the full strength of that small word. We have to qualify it, make reservations and conditions, for if we did not, we should have to imply that the subject of that small verb had no limitation conceivable, that the thought of its opposite, " is not," must be utterly ruled out. We are told in legends of springs which are never exhausted, of sacred fires which burn without loss and inconsumedly and supply the flame to all other lights. Such images serve to convey the idea I want to enforce, the lack of inner vigour and overflowing energy which characterizes everything finite, and the necessity therefore for the existence of some infinitely rich source which never fails and can never be supplemented —and it is this source which deserves the name of God.

Thus starting with what every man of common sense demands, to wit, that the happenings before his eyes should have a beginning and a cause, we have passed to a more scientific and philosophical argument, by which it appears that there must be some originator and cause, which itself is uncaused because it necessarily exists and is so supreme and complete as to need no outside assistance or condition to be what it is. In simpler language, the universe and all its contents present themselves to us as tenants, as existing on a lease, temporary or perpetual, and their tenure depends on a proprietor who owes nothing to any man and exists by right divine. Of course, this argument has not gone without opposition; it has been challenged again and again, and it is only fair that I should mention the grounds of its rejection. They vary, however, in a disconcerting way. Many critics do not formulate any precise objection; their reluctance to yield assent is due rather to a suspicion that " it can't be as easy as all that ". They fear a trick somewhere, and if the argument is put in an abstract way it does not seem to correspond with what they believe or want. They have, too, little confidence in philosophy as their minds have been fuddled, or if that is too harsh a word, confused by the triumphs of science. Those who do formulate their objections follow the same lines. They argue that science is the only possible form of knowledge which is sure and science has nothing to say about God, and they may go on to protest that metaphysics is just jargon. If they are acquainted with the latest forms of scientific method, they will add that the word, cause, has fallen into disrepute, that it is not used in the physical sciences, and that long ago Hume buried it under his criticism.

This is the kind of objection which by being quoted or mentioned has caused a number of well-meaning people to doubt the force of the arguments and call themselves agnostics. Now it is always more difficult to answer an objection than to propound it. If I were to say that I had never understood how one could come to the end of space as I could not step off it if there were no more space to fall into, my listeners would realize that the difficulty was a childish one, but they would be hard put to it to answer me in terms suited to the style of the objection. Similarly, with difficulties which have been raised against the classical arguments for the existence of God. I must ask readers therefore, if they do not care for abstruse discussion, to skip the next few paragraphs, as it is impossible to avoid some technical philosophy in replying to the difficulties I have enumerated.

Most of the difficulties can be traced back to Hume or Kant; the remainder may be said to express that mood of uncertainty and diffidence which is so prevalent as to deserve some attention. Hume introduced into philosophy what has now become known as Scotch caution. He would not go beyond admitting that we did get impressions from outside things and that most of our so-called knowledge might be called a lively faith in or expectation of the future being like the past. The result of his caution was that there seemed no room in reality for substances, causes, persons or philosophy properly so called. The fatal effect of such teaching was realized by Kant, who also had some Scotch blood in his veins, and his efforts were directed to restoring some of the convictions of common sense and justifying science which had been paralysed by the criticisms of Hume. Kant, therefore, taught that our notions of cause and law, our inductions and generalizations were justified so long as we restricted them to the world we know by our senses, in other words, the world which is the subject matter of the physical sciences. We are fed by sensation and we digest them in accordance with our mental make up. We do not just passively and contentedly receive impressions through our senses of the external world, nor is it any use for us to try to speculate without the help of sensible experience. Our mental digestive organs need their food as much as our physical ones, and what has been called metaphysics is an unprogressive science for the reason that it expresses the attempt to think beyond sensible experience, to formulate truths without any content.

Both these views rule out the possibility of proving the existence of God, as their authors freely admitted, and so popular did they become that gradually it was taken for granted among intelligent groups of men and women that the way to prove God's existence had been finally closed. Only the professional thinkers could remember what exactly were the views of Hume and Kant and what arguments Kant used to expose the ancient proofs, and even among these professional thinkers few accepted the general position of Kant. They followed their own lights, but when it came to the question of God they hurried over the subject with a brief reference to the annihilating character of the Kantian objections or a hasty repetition of them, and then passed on to what they thought more alive and interesting. It was no wonder that the reading public were persuaded to believe that indeed theology had ceased to be a science. Nevertheless, this belief is quite mistaken, as the objections which are thought to be so destructive rest almost entirely on the theories of the two philosophers already mentioned and stand or fall with the truth of these theories. There are few nowadays who follow Kant, and the scepticism of Hume is such that if it were tolerated there would be an end to all science and all serious human intercourse.

As it is Kant who expressly formulated what he took to be the flaws in the proofs for God's existence, let us examine them. Kant had maintained that our knowledge cannot go beyond the boundaries of the sensible world and that therefore the existence of an infinite God could not be deduced from the finite. When then the theist argues from the existence of the contingent to the existence of an absolute, necessary being, a nest of contradiction can be found in his argument. What is here spoken of as absolute is nothing more than a necessary and limiting condition, a sign indeed of the limitation of our power of thinking but in no way guaranteeing any real object possessing any content. That such a necessary being should be identified with a single and perfect one is a conclusion far beyond the premisses. There is indeed a concealed premiss in the argument which is nothing else than the famous ontological assumption. This ontological argument which St. Anselm was the first to state explicitly runs as follows. I can conceive a being than which nothing greater can be conceived. But if such a being were merely a conception or idea in my head it would be less than a being which existed not only in my head but in actual fact; in other words, a being which existed would be more perfect than one which did not; therefore the greatest being conceivable of which I can think must exist. This is such a peculiar argument and sounds so like a quibble that generation after generation of thinkers has written about it. Most have rejected it, though the fact that they chose different reasons for doing so suggests that they have not been altogether happy that they had found the flaw. Kant thought the fallacy to be in treating existence as if it were a perfection on a par with other qualities of a thing or person. His point is that to your definition of, say, twenty shillings or a man it does not make any difference whether they exist or not. A scientist can define an extinct species of animal, a plesiosaurus or mammoth for example, and obviously it makes no difference to the meaning of a thing whether it be walking about or only preserved in a museum. The modern logicians make the same point when they show that the propositions " dogs bite " and " dogs exist " cannot be analysed in the same way. The first is translated into, " if any dogs exist they all bite," while the second should mean " if any dogs exist they all exist," a proposition which is merely tautologous. I do not say that these modern logicians are themselves talking sense when they proceed this way, but all are satisfied that the ontological argument is fallacious.

Having agreed that this is so they then in the wake of Kant reject the chief of the classical arguments for the existence of God as also fallacious, because, as they say, it contains in it the ontological fallacy. Let me repeat this argument in the shortest form possible. There are in existence beings which are contingent; that is to say, we discover with our minds beings which we are bound to say do not necessarily exist; but if such beings do not exist of their own right and by their definition, they must depend on something else. This something else again either depends upon itself for its existence or it does not; if the first we have already arrived at a being whose existence is necessary, self-constituted and self-dependent; if the second, then it in turn could not be existing were it not dependent on something else. Now whether one goes on in this way to infinity or not, not one of the series could be there at all if there be not a necessary being, any more than a series of sneezes even though they be infinite in number could be sneezes at all were there no organism or body already in existence. It follows that there must be a being who necessarily exists and this we call God. Where now in this argument does the ontological lie concealed? The supposed fallacy in that argument consists in this, that out of the mere idea of a perfect being the real existence of one is deduced on the plea that otherwise the being conceived would not be perfect. Search as one may, there is nothing like this in the proof which has just been outlined. It started not with an idea but with observed or known real existent beings and from these existent beings it offers to show that a necessary or self-existent being exists.

The truth is that Kant has been looking for a mare's nest and that he has translated the old proof into his own terms and his own philosophy and then turned round and said that it does not hold. On his view the mind is helpless unless it confines itself to what is based on sensible experience. When, therefore, it takes flight into regions beyond experience the ideas it conceives are without content. They may serve as ideal limits and that is all. God if this be true can, therefore, be nothing more than a horizon of our thinking—a limit we impose, and we have no right to make a substance of such a limit and assert its existence. He thinks this is to pass from an idea to its reality. But such a view rests entirely on his assumption that no idea can transcend experience and this is demonstrably false. For one thing we cannot think of experience without transcending it, and if we really can know anything there can be no reason, from the point of view of knowledge, why knowing should not include everything. Moreover, one cannot limit knowledge this way without in the very doing of it going beyond the limitation. Kant's inability to make a coherent statement and analysis of his own theory is its best refutation. Are we, however, to reject as peremptorily his next objection to the effect that the classical proof identifies arbitrarily a necessary and a perfect being? It may be true that at a first glance they may not seem identical, but a short consideration will show that they must be the same. If a being is necessary by its own internal constitution, it must possess within it so much power that it needs not anything else whatsoever for its vigorous existence, and what can that mean save that what it is must be so perfect that it cannot wane or suffer diminution or be disturbed by anything external to it ; in other words, that what has been described in negative terms as indefectibility is rightly described positively as perfection, the complete realization of all that contains no weakness. And if it be asked further whether such a being must necessarily be unique and singular, the answer is and must be straightway in the affirmative, seeing that two such beings would require some relation to each other and such a relation would imply something in one which the other did not possess.

For these reasons and many others the kind of criticism which has been handed down by Kant must be dismissed as irrelevant. Let us therefore turn to other possible difficulties. Some of these have been already mentioned. They can be sorted out as of three kinds ; the one says that the finite cannot bear witness to the infinite ; it can tell us no more than is required to explain the finite ; the second says that we have no right to suppose that the universe is really intelligible. There are dark spaces to it ; there are surds which are of their nature insoluble ; there is no relation between the suffering of a particular man, the sound of a banjo and the existence of mathematics. We cannot, that is, fit into a neat scheme all the constituents and all happenings, past, present and future; we are even uncertain whether any particular facts can be deduced from their antecedents like a conclusion of an addition or multiplication sum. The third difficulty is not so very unlike the other two, but it is perhaps less sophisticated, for it echoes the complaint of the multitude that these high speculations always seem very fragile and a little unreal and that at the end of them so little of the God we wish to hear about has been learnt that the knowledge is almost worthless.

These difficulties can be dealt with summarily. The first is only specious, for why should not the finite witness to the infinite? It is a mere prejudice to say that it cannot do so. We might as well say that a bodily movement can only be explained by a bodily cause and that, therefore, we can never argue to a cause like the human will. The truth is that just as certain bodily movements give evidence within them of a power which is purposeful, so too certain finite actions or beings bear within them the evidence that only a complete being could have been ultimately responsible for them. Or again if we saw a number of concave surfaces we should not be impressed by the argument of a man who said that to deduce the presence also of something convex was going beyond the evidence, as all that we saw was concave. When we consider objects around us we find as part of their reality that they are contingent; they tell us something about themselves which implies that they could not be what they are, any more than a concave could be such without the convex, unless a non-contingent being also existed. We have therefore taken no step beyond the evidence in declaring the existence of a necessary being. It is our opponent who wishes to close all possibility of knowing God by asserting that the visible world cannot testify to Him, and it is he who begs the question by such dogmatism and refuses to weigh the evidence.

The second difficulty looks less plausible but is more serious—at any rate against certain opponents. There is on the one hand our system of thinking which is happiest when it is dealing with mathematics, that system, that is, which connects abstract sums and equations and propositions together by a kind of necessity. The most conspicuous examples are the geometries which have been invented, and amongst philosophies the schemes of Spinoza and Hegel. The philosophy of Hegel has often been called the logic of life, and its opponents have exclaimed against its stuffiness, complaining that it suffocated freedom and all that intimate and incalculable variety which we see around us in nature and in human happenings. If thought so flattens out life, what right, we may go on to ask, have we to suppose that the universe, seen as in a mist, really corresponds with thought? Surely it is likely that there are many parts of it which cannot be fitted together into a thought pattern, that, in fact, much of it may be unintelligible! And if this be so, then the proof for the existence of God which contained the concealed premiss that the universe was intelligible is thoroughly mistaken. Such is the difficulty, and, as I say, it is serious if what I have just written be true. Fortunately the proofs for the existence of God have little or nothing to do with the Hegelian system or any other system which pretends that human thinking fits the world like a glove. To make the theistic and Christian position clear we must distinguish carefully between the two statements that the world is intelligible and that the world is fully intelligible to us. It is nonsense to deny that the world is intelligible; such a denial implies that there could be something which could in no way be noticed or recognized or known by anyone to be what it is. Notice that this is not a question of saying that it might not be knowable by us, that it is too fine for human senses, too profound for human investigation; such a state of affairs is not only likely but certainly true. But we are going far further than that and now pretending to ourselves that some things which are unknown to us are of such a nature that they are utterly unknowable, and that not by our minds alone but by any mind whatsoever. Such a statement is, as I have said, just words with no meaning attached, for thing and intelligible are interchangeable terms. If they were not then we would go wrong with the very first term we used, seeing that by thing we must include anything and mean to include anything. If it were not

147

really all inclusive, our statement would be wrong, and it would follow that everything else we said would also be wrong, as all statements and all knowledge depend on some foundation; even the principle of contradiction would become a conjecture applicable to the reality which we suppose, without certainty, we have discovered. Indeed, all would be turned topsy-turvy.

In denying that there can be a part of reality which no intelligence could know, we are, therefore, defending the intelligence from a charge of imbecility. But it is not enough to make this denial; we must go on to show the real case which lies behind the objection. And here the third objection will serve as a clue. So much is, in fact, dark to us that many scientists and philosophers are frankly sceptical about the powers of the human intelligence, and if the Hegels try to construct a rounded whole of knowledge, the Bergsons flout it as a mere instrument which gets in the way as much as it serves. When then the critics compare the chessboard of science with the unchanging face of the world they succumb to the temptation to conclude that reality may well be so different from any system of thought that it is wrong to build upon their happy agreement. What they should have said is that though reality must be intelligible it does unfortunately lose a dimension when mirrored in human thought. This implies both that human thought gives us a true picture of reality and also that it is through "a dark mirror" and feeble in vision; and this is precisely the theistic position, that attitude of modesty and assurance which has been verified throughout the development of science and civilization. The Christian theist rejects the apotheosis of human reason and points to the failure of Spinoza and Hegel as one proof of his belief; he will not, however, scorn the gift of God, the gift which has made him like to God and capable of knowing something of the truth of the world and himself and reaching out to a vision of absolute perfection in truth and beauty and goodness.

We are back again at the conclusions reached in a former chapter and are taught once more the lesson of a humility which enlivens and does not depress. We can know that God exists and that with Him and in Him abide the standards of perfection which we dimly apprehend. We can even see that in some mysterious way He must unite in Himself all that beauty which we discern parcelled out and subdued to imperfection around us. It is enough for the moment to know that there is a higher order towards which we may climb with the help of the power above. The truth of our own infirmity is salutary and is a necessary prelude to what by God's bounty has been vouchsafed to us in the Christian revelation. Most of the thoughts which run in our mind and most of the information we possess have come to us from parents, teachers and reading. Man, as the first political thinker said, is a social animal; he is himself in a family and in a state. In infancy he is more feeble than the cub or spawn, and the history of the word idiot exhibits how prized and necessary is social intercourse. If then even on that level where he runs most easily he is all the time dependent on co-operation, are we to suppose that man can become a member of the city of God, of the " region yonder " without assistance from on high ?

I have sketched the form which our knowledge must take when it essays to comprehend God and the inaccessible light in which He dwells. We may compare it to an early map of the Americas with a few meagre lines—so different from the reality ; or again to the grey prospect of an explorer when he sees a world before him with league on league of snow and ice-bound land. It looks dead and monotonous and its far silence conveys no message to his frozen body. And yet this grim and unharvestable land may, when spring has passed and the summer sun has relaxed its snows, bring gladness to the heart of the patient and rich plenty from its yellow fields and overladen trees. This life-giving and nourishing nature, celebrated under so many names in ancient myth, the goddess who must be wooed by labour and with patience is a symbol of One who is hidden from our eyes and is hidden behind the works of His hands. He is too vast to fit into any pattern of our knowledge, too close to be felt in the tumult of our sensations. He has not however left Himself without evidence in nature, and He has made

Himself small so that He might come within the focus of human sight, that thus through our weakness He might lift mankind up to heights where He can be beheld in undiminished splendour.

CHAPTER IV

THE CHRISTIAN IDEAL

S O far we have been engaged in testing some of the alternatives to the Christian ideal which have been put forward at one time or another, and in a former chapter I have tried to show that clouds gather and hide truth, goodness and beauty if we look for them apart from a personal God and immortality. It is now time to consider whether the Christian ideal is true and satisfying and beautiful. Many would say that it is not and for many different reasons. Brewster, for instance, thought that definite faiths, such as the Christian, were too schematic and too limited. They are the products of the brain and lie before one like a chessboard, a pattern of conceptual squares, as dull as any multiplication table. His desire is to get away from himself, and time and time again he finds the shadow where he had hoped that he had left it behind. The formulas of the Christian Creed are for him essentially human, and that is their condemnation. To many others it is religion, and especially the Christian religion which is unreal. This world is the only one we know and we want happiness here, and all the mythology about the supernatural is an impediment or " the opium of the people."

The answer to such diverse criticisms is best given, perhaps, by a true portrait of Christianity. We shall then be in the position to appreciate the objections to it, and I must ask my readers to be indulgent when I try to condense into a few pages the manifold splendour of the Christian scheme of life. In the *Antigone* of Sophocles the chorus sings that " there are many and wondrous things, but there is naught more wonderful than man." This legitimate exaggeration repeats itself ever and ever again across the pages of human history ; he is ever at work trying to express himself, in deeds of courage and adventure, in the trades and arts, in his relations with his fellows and with nature, in poetry and story and in books of self-analysis and cosmic theories. As he grew to know himself better through the records of others and intercourse, he came to see that his distinctness lay in the possession of mind. By having a mind he was a person separate from inanimate things and from animals, in that he could know himself to some extent, be a king within the domain of himself, control his fancy and imagination, be free both from external compulsion and to choose good or bad. These powers and prerogatives conferred on him what has come to be called personality. A person stands off from other things and is not a part of nature ; he is self-determining and can even impose his will on the world. This is the reason that man has maintained a proud spirit throughout

his history and gone from success to success in explora-
tion and in the subjugation of nature, in the advance of
science and development of social relations.

On the other hand, he has also been disquieted by the
transitory nature of his life—the kind of disquiet lying
behind the words, " the glories of our blood and state
are shadows not substantial things "—by the fragility
and crookedness of much so-called freedom, and the
skein of darkness, like a cataract in the eye, which covers
the laborious and slow-working efforts of the mind in
scientific and philosophic investigation. In this systole
and diastole lies the secret of man's nature, and alone of
all philosophies the Christian has taken it fully into
account. A ready and correct answer, so far as it goes,
will ascribe this peculiarity of the human character to the
union of soul and body, but very few are able to develop
this distinction rightly. The Christian has already the
clue in the Psalms and sapiential books of the Old
Testament. " What is man that thou art mindful of
him ? . . . For thou hast made him but little lower
than God, . . . thou madest him to have dominion over
the works of thy hands ; thou hast put all things under
his feet." Here we have stated the excellence of man
and his position in this universe. He is the overseer of
material creation and he is so because he is like in some
degree to the Supreme Spirit. He has been made the
high priest of a world which awaits his ministry before
it can divulge its meaning and join in a cosmic hymn to
its Creator. The mountains are but masses of stone,

the rivers and sea fluid matter, the flowers a chemical composition, the stars senseless blobs until their significance is picked out of them by a spirit which gives them names, is fascinated by their beauty and rejoices in the discovery of their laws and natures. They rise up into life in his thought of them and man can carry in his mind and soul the distilled perfection of a now wondrous universe. This is man's task and function; he is kin by his body to what is physical; his senses take in the colour and shape and sound of all around him, and his mind, aloof and superior, can reckon up the gifts brought to it by the senses. Nor is it just passive to what it receives. Pulsing with activity it flushes the sensible experience and views it *sub specie aeternitatis*, in the medium of those absolute standards and forms which as Wordsworth felt are the intimates of soul from childhood. The soul of man bears the imprint and likeness of its creator and every experience sets re-echoing the music of divine beauty; truth takes form there in the guise of human wisdom, and the self thus adorned becomes more and more precious and knows itself a person.

It is in this setting that we can best understand the Christian religion. Instead of the vague and abstract language about truth and goodness we are to think of a Person or more accurately a Being with personality who possesses these characters in a way which makes them identical with Him. Something of His nature, while it escapes our human standards, can nevertheless be conceived by the help of our own nature and personality. Whereas we are limited monarchs within our own domain and still more limited in our suzerainty over the universe, this Being will have none of those limitations which obscure the vigour and comeliness of human nature ; and if we are vital and loving He will be the mainspring of love and goodness. All that we have is derived ; our nature is a rough sketch in a weak medium of some perfection which it suggests, and as spirit springs from spirit, as thought from thought, not by inches or by loss and gain, man can be said to come from God whole and entire in its own order. If we ask why God should thus make an inferior type to imitate the glorious prototype which is Himself, the question can have no adequate answer. It is, in fact, an impossible question, for God is not in want of anything nor is He to be thought of as acting for the sake of some good which He does not possess. Our notion of generosity comes nearest to an answer because generosity has no ulterior motive ; it is love superabundant which sweeps away all questioning. But if some explanation must be tried, then let us say that creation exemplifies the truth which holds amongst us that the more perfect a man or woman is the more does he or she tend to give just for the sake of giving. And the result of God's love is ourselves. The love we all have for our own welfare, the profound instinct for self-preservation, the pathetic fallacy which makes us live to see our own death and all that will be recorded of us, these are clear pointers to the necessity from our point of view (not from God's) that we should have been created. So fixed is this in the human mind that systems of Idealism have been invented which declare that the whole world depends for its existence on our beholding of it ; and if to many it sounds comic that a " tree ceases to be when there is no one about in the quad," we should remember that such a belief has often occurred to man and is a witness of the price he puts upon himself.

Accusations against fate or God are the expression usually not so much of the desire for total disappearance as of disappointment, and this disappointment, it can be argued, shows that man has high expectations and takes himself seriously. He carries a baton in his spiritual knapsack and he takes for granted, until events gainsay his wishes, that the stars will fight in their courses for him, that " God is in His heaven and all is well with the world." Soon alas ! he discovers that his desires are often checkmated and that he is severely handicapped. I have begun to give what I think to be the truth about man and God and the relations between them, but it would be foolish to suppose that man reaches them spontaneously and securely. The wise and intelligent for centuries were maddened by their inability to capture in their thought the message and meaning of nature, themselves and God. Maddening indeed is it to have a mind and to be a self, and yet when that self comes to be examined to find that it slips away like quicksilver ; to look upon nature and discover that very little turns out to be what its appearance suggests. and to use the

name of God and to suffer from stupor and imbecility
when asked to explain the meaning of the sacred name.
To know nature only superficially, and to know neither
God nor oneself, this is a strange and tantalizing condition. Nevertheless, it is that of man, and the recognition of this fact is the necessary propædeutic to the Christian religion. At the time when Christ came the knowledge of man had already advanced to a high level and
men were conscious of their powers and their weaknesses.
To many the result could be summed up in the image
of the Sphinx which answered with riddles and was
impenetrable.

Why this light and darkness? Why this paradox
that human beings should be able to conceive faintly
of the best and have no strength to follow it? The
Christian answers that the relations between God and
man had been interrupted with the consequence that
man left to his own devices had stumbled on darkness.
If man is endowed with intellect and self-determination,
with eternal wisdom to be his vernacular tongue, tenant
on earth and destined to immortal mansions, then we
should expect that much would be required of him.
His very excellence brought with it a high responsibility,
and just because the love of God set infinite greatness
within his grasp the failure to respond to such an invitation was bound to be disastrous. In other words, if we
take seriously what man has thought of himself, even
what he has achieved of grandeur at certain moments,
then we may be sure that God will be inflexible in

demanding the highest of him and in refusing to tolerate anything below it. Such treatment is to man's best interests ultimately, and it is the law of love as well as justice. What therefore more likely, even if we did not know it to be so from Revelation, than that the first proper act of man should be a test, a cosmic decision, wherein he should have to make up his mind whether God or self should come first, a choice of his free will, helped with the love and grace of God, between the majesty which he, a petty king, seemed to possess and the humility requisite if he were to be brought into union with God Himself?

That he chose wrongly is known from Revelation and it is written across the pages of his history. His mind suffered a shock similar to that which the psycho-analysts would have us believe can happen to children. The memory is dimmed and human beings can no longer think clearly of what is associated with the original experience. The mind suffers vertigo when it dwells on what is the most high, and it can succeed only by using numbed and insensible abstractions. The will, too, feeling no longer the fiery darts of divine love and quickened instead by the senses and earthly passions is in desperate straits to resist the latter and follow the summons of cold duty. We are all, nevertheless, haunted by perfection, and we all long for some golden occasion when we can exhibit our strength, write down for all time what we are and could be and so wipe out the long array of petty deeds which go under our name.

I said that the intercourse between God and man was interrupted. That is only partially true, for in reality the love of God never slackened. What is true is that God had to leave man to his own devices and make that experience part of His new plan of love. *Vae soli !* By the bitter experience of living and depending on himself man would learn that the choice he had made led to unhappiness, and through the very evil he had brought down upon himself God would bring back union.

It is to be noticed that throughout the history of mankind God has taken man on his own terms, so much so that His providence has hidden itself in the works of nature and the free acts of each individual. This instead of causing vexation and surprise should strike us as a new courtesy on the part of God and a new light upon His esteem for human nature. God has allowed Himself to be dictated to by His creatures, to treat with them solely on the terms of their free choices. His Universe is distorted and made ugly, His Name is tossed to and fro and made into an expletive and He is banished from His own kingdom. That out of human choices and human error and culpability He can draw felicity and by submitting His love to the frail guidance of human wills He can yet with overmastering skill accomplish His designs, this for those who consider it carefully is far more wonderful—if more painful for us—than the exercise of omnipotence without regard for the laws of nature and of life. The supreme evidence of this attitude is seen in the primary dogmas of the Christian religion.

There we learn that God, having trained the Jews to be prepared for His coming and having left the other races of the world to learn by experience the misfortune of rejecting God's help and relying on their own strength, became a man like unto ourselves. " That the great angel-blinding Light should shrink his blaze to shine in a poor shepherd's eye," that the remote, all-encompassing power felt with fear and awe by the children of men at birth and death, in storm and in dark places should be seen in a cradle and amid the fields of corn, this fairy dream must be accepted as historical truth. There is the evidence of eye-witnesses to the man, and there is the evidence of the miracles, of the teaching and the character and the risen Christ to the claim to divinity.

But the limitations, the very difficulty in believing the record of this life and its ending are, so to speak, the expression made external of the desires and will of man. Just as our desires, so we are told by doctors, image themselves forth in the dreams of the night, and just as the broken palaces, the memorials scattered over the earth, are the external featuring of the human will, so what we know of God in Christ's suffering is man's achievement. But this time it is not a fairy tale, as I have said, not the drama in words of a Sophocles or Shakespeare, but a desire come to life by the response of God to the wants and the determination of man, epitomized in the Jew. " He became obedient, taking the form of a servant." He was royal, but the defilement of royalty had made it impossible for Him to act the king;

He was wisdom, but the scribblings of supposedly wise man had made Him converse in parables; He was love, but the loves in which men had indulged made Him fierce and intolerant; He was victor, but His victory had to come through the shame of the Cross.

Thus it was that man made divinity shape his ends. Let it not be thought, however, that in saying this the Christian dogma has any likeness to that of those who go about saying that Christianity is a fair fable and that the Christ of religion is nothing more than a projection of our desires. There have been many fables, and they usually betray their too human origin. The lower nature we possess is only too evident in the loves of the Greek gods and the obscenities which have crept into the oriental religions. But purify them of all that is distasteful and admire their glimpses of a god of love and mercy, their passion stories, their dramas of divine reconciliation; they do indeed express the longing of the human soul, but they remain fabulous and vague like a wrack of clouds dissolving into an empty firmament. Compared with the truth they have the unsubstantiality of dreams, and they cease to have meaning just where the Christian revelation gives a logos of the infinite. The human gods of the fables are creatures of the imagination like centaurs, the trinities have no unity and are nothing more than a convenient division of a mysterious divine nature into so many *dramatis personæ*, whereas in the Christ there are threaded together mystery and the deepest thought and experience, and in the Christian

Trinity the one God reveals a new marvel of the possibility of love superabounding within itself and without divorce.

But it is in the Atonement that the Christian religion rises into its dazzling splendour. To the Gentile, as St. Paul said, it was folly, " to the Jews a stumbling-block, but to those who believe the power and the wisdom of God." By belief here St. Paul does not mean a private emotional experience which the sober heads would name superstition; he means the difference between the Pharisee who saw a man on a cross and the centurion who with the same scene before him saw God, and that it is our " estranged faces that miss the many splendoured thing." On an external and superficial aspect the dogma of the Atonement is the interpretation put upon the story of a man Christ who was crucified by his own people and was reported to have risen from the dead—let us say, therefore, the slaying by the Jews of their greatest prophet and an empty tomb. The traditional religious interpretation of it is that this Christ sacrificed Himself for His people and the world and so made atonement for sin to God. To understand it further we must however fall back on the principle I have already stated, that God's love works through the intentions of man and completes his understanding. Now amongst these intentions or, let us say, ways of looking at things, injury, punishment, satisfaction and forgiveness play an immemorial part. Moreover, in relation to the forces which control life these phases take on the nature of sacrifice. No doubt sacrifice is best explained as the natural expression of homage of a creature in presence of its maker, but the form which that sacrifice has taken has passed through the whole gamut of emotions of which man is capable. Sacrifice, therefore, being the way we all take when wrongdoing and reparation are in question, the symbol and the reality of God's intercourse with man and man's treatment of Him are embodied and shown forth in sacrifice ; and the wisdom, if we may so dare speak, of God is proved by the fact that the crucifix can be understood by everyone, from the most simple to the wisest, that it has always struck home to the religious mind in a unique manner, and that it condenses all that can be thought and desired in one outstanding representation.

All this goes to confirm the statement formerly made that man dictates to God the manner in which God will act, the while God's love triumphs through these very limitations, and this truth is seen in shining glory in the Redemption. The human act, like the Holy Grail or the blood of St. Januarius, changes as we look upon it, and what was human in appearance glows red with divinity. The lowest level of understanding is seen in the barbaric notion that God being angry with mankind for its evil doing maltreats the innocent because His lust for punishment must be sated. This travesty of the truth appears occasionally in anti-religious literature. More noble is the view that an innocent and pure victim substitutes himself for the guilty and acts as their ransom.

The idea imbedded in this view is too close to human nature to be altogether wrong. Incident after incident from fable and history shows its appeal to some instinct in us, and indeed there can be no question of the virtue of the victim who freely takes the place of his guilty friends. What troubles us in the transaction is not the valour and generosity of the man, but the willingness of God to let an innocent man be punished in place of the guilty. So long as the innocent and the guilty are entirely separate, we are left dissatisfied and God's action remains strange. But the whole action is changed if the sufferer be God Himself become man for the love of men, and if the divine love be so responsive to human demands that God " empties Himself," becoming truly a man. This Son of Man is not a substitute; the assumption of manhood makes Him one with all the guilty, as their representative, their head and perfection and the principle of a new life. Love dominates the whole proceeding, making it unfold a whole new train of divine events. Love identifies the Lord of life with a race which by its refusal and pride had checked the movement of man into a life of absolute truth and goodness. This incarnate Love works out the fatal choice of man, takes all that we have decided to be and expresses it once for all in a cosmic act which sums up the results of our conduct. Each man, we are told, slays the thing he loves, and the better self which God has offered us takes shape in the figure on a cross. But before this shattering spectacle can reduce us to the despair of an

Othello, the eye of faith bids us see that it is divine love which is suffering and that this divine love by that very act of self-sacrifice has lifted us into union with itself.

This is the last stage of the mystery. "But God (who is rich in mercy) for his exceeding charity wherewith he loved us even when we were dead in sins, hath quickened us together with Christ." That is to say that just as the death of the God-Man was a representative act, incorporating in it all that we have and are—no mere substitution but identification—so the victory in death, the splendour surrounding the divine humility and love, belongs to all those who now accept this new divine offer. That this is no fanciful interpretation the words of the greatest of theologians set forth in their own quiet technical language will show. By the Passion

man learns how much God loves man ; and by it he incited to that return of love in which the perfection of our human salvation consists. . . . Secondly, because by it he gave us an example of obedience, humility, constancy, justice and the other virtues displayed in the Passion. . . . Thirdly, because Christ by his Passion not only freed man from sin but merited for him justifying grace and the glory of beatitude as will be explained later. . . .

What that explanation is the simplest Christian child knows, namely, that we are reborn into a new life in the death of Christ, that in the words of the Fourth Gospel, " he came unto his own and his own received him not, but to as many as received him he gave power to be the sons of God." The divine life which was Christ's by natural right he confers on all who become his members and accept his grace. To develop this further would be to begin the theology of grace, and many may be familiar with it or at least think that they know its main assertions. Sufficient therefore will it be to suggest this way of approaching the subject, so often misunderstood, of Catholic teaching. This, at any rate, ought to be clear, that the surface meaning of the Atonement is only a hint of the depths which lie beneath, and if we wish for a clue to the marvellous story of Christ we must begin by remembering that He has lowered Himself to our level and that it is by starting there that we shall be most likely to reach onwards to the inner significance of His life.

I recall this hint for two reasons. The first is that only by such means does it seem possible that a religion could be universal, and the second that by bearing it in mind we shall be able to see the injustice of the criticism which has been brought against Christianity by those who would fly higher. Few of us stop to consider how almost impossible it would appear that a religion should be pure and exalted and at the same time universal. Nevertheless, the difficulty is obvious and has made itself felt fatally in almost all if not all religions except Christianity. As all know the Hindoo belief as developed by its sages is lofty and profound, though to many of us it loses itself in the sands of speculation. On the other hand, the popular cult is accompanied by much that is abhorrent and seems to be a dissolute counterfeit

of the inner teaching, and what holds true of this eastern
religion is paralleled in the worship of Greece and
Rome. The populace and the élite will never agree in
their tastes, and whereas the man in the street or in the
fields is quickened only by imagery and by an appeal
to his emotions, the student and the recluse prefer to
discard what they call the deceptive trappings of sense.
God who wills the salvation of all men would, it seems,
be forced, too, to make the way easy if He is to take
into consideration the childishness of so many and the
sensual and selfish inclinations of the majority of the
human race. And yet if He were to act on this plea
how could He face the criticism which would immediately arise to the effect that God's ideal for man is not
even as noble as what human beings have been able to
invent for themselves? We can then imagine the
dilemma of God : either I announce an ideal which is
worthy of its divine author, and then I must make it so
exalted and arduous that only the few will be able to
attempt it, or I must take into account the weakness of
the multitudes and ordain a rule of life so easy that it
will fall short of the best which man himself can conceive
and be unworthy of Me. Moreover, if this ideal is to
be universal it must be capable of translation into the
idiom of countless races in every age with their changing
tastes and desires, their varying cultures and philosophies.
The South Sea Islander worshipping before his wooden
idol is to have the same religion as the admirer of
Hegel, and the girl behind the counter in Woolworth's

as the Oscar Wildes and Cézannes.   Truly, as the prophet
said, the wolf is to lie down with the lamb !   Thus we
are to have a religion which is so graded that without
loss to its integrity it can appeal to every type of man,
the simple and the profound, the barbarian and the
sophisticated, the introvert and the extrovert, the matter-
of-fact and the romantic, the conventional and the odd,
those who have to see before they can think and those
who prefer to think before they will see.

Moreover, this religion must have no chinks in its
armour ; it must be armed cap-à-pie.   This means that
it must be the last word in truth and at the same time
open out infinite vistas for the mystics to see and rejoice
thereat, and in addition it must gather all, these mystics
included, into a unity which in its mutual love and
singleness of purpose will surpass that of any family
gathering.   And as if this were not already too much
the beauty and truth of that religion must float like a
visible banner before all and be capable of transformation into vivid, coloured, sensuous form.   A religion
which neglects the senses is doomed to failure for the
simple reason that men and women in all the major
concerns of life, whether it be lovemaking or the forma-
tion of city and community life, are stirred by what they
can see and feel and touch.   A reasoned philosophy
without any condiment can never be a universal religion ;
a revivalist appeal which depends mainly on the emotions
dies almost as soon as it is born ; the mystic who sings
outside all choruses cannot command a company, and

the meistersingers who prefer custom and rule to any
new inspiration and rely on organization as an end in
itself suffocate others and are in time suffocated themselves.

I know of only one religion which even remotely
approaches the demands just laid down, and that is the
Christian religion. Were this the occasion to make a
defence of it I should spend some time trying to show
how closely knitted together are the three requisites just
named. It is intellectual, in this sense at least, that it
never leaves its dogmas covered with wool; it sets
them forth and tries to show in theological language
taken from the best thought of the world that they
are the product of a supreme wisdom and logically flaw-
less. The insistence which this religion places on the
truth inscribed in dogma does not prevent it, nevertheless, from giving full scope for the mystics who have
ever abounded within it, and these dogmas are translated into ever-varying and coloured symbols and rites,
which are controlled by the truth to be expressed ; and,
lastly, the abstractions of the intellect are made living in
the Word made flesh, Divinity made visible in the form
of a man who was seen and touched. It is in Christ
and by Christ that all which otherwise might have seemed
impossible is accomplished, and just because He is a
man as well as God, able to speak in a human language
which nevertheless draws from the unsoundable riches
of eternity, His message of truth is not checked by time
or space, by undue learning or undue simplicity, by

changes in custom and culture, by love of the visible image or love of the invisible. If Christ be God, then it is possible for God to manifest Himself through the veil of flesh, and it follows that the highest truth too can be so shaded for the childish mind of man that it can be at the disposal of all. One condition is required, that the sensuous devotions, the emotional appeals, the imagery and the pageantry and all that goes to aid the half-paralysed intellect to raise itself to the spiritual should be controlled by dogma. If once these various mediums become detached from the truth they are there to exhibit, then the images rapidly become idols and the devotion superstition.

Another way of putting this distinction of Christianity is to say that it alone can concentrate and forward life. Christ said that He came to give life and that more abundantly, and however difficult it may be to define what we mean by life, there can be no doubt that all else, thought, artistic or mystic experience, happiness, are to be judged by its increase. We cannot by taking thought add one cubit to our stature, and neither story nor the best thought-out philosophy or conversation can serve as an adequate deputy. That is the reason why people tire of speculation and taking things at second-hand. The life which is ours is manifested in our instincts and in our longings, and it includes all, every part of us, in its growth. This growth is what concerns each one of us individually, and we know not what we are and what we may become. The God we can conceive of must draw near and touch us by His presence. He must be to us not what a cold idea is dwelling in the mind, not the *Deus absconditus* but a God of love who gives increase to our elfin love and life. Such a visitant takes us by surprise and sweeps aside our protestations of strength or weakness in order to envelop both in His understanding of what we are. As Pascal has said, there are two schools of supposed wisdom which would feed the soul and end by leaving it famished and dying; " the one knowing man's duties and ignoring his helplessness, is lost in presumption, whilst the other, knowing his helplessness and not his duty, falls into cowardice. . . ." Neither of these can give life, and I quote these words of Pascal because they illustrate the error of all those who have been mentioned as proposing a more excellent way than that of Christianity.

I have said that the second reason for starting with the " emptying " or humility of Christ was that it helped us to see the errors of those who proposed this more excellent way. It might be said that their errors can be marked down without any preliminary fuss, and I admit readily that most of the alternatives to the Christian ideal do turn out, when scrutinized carefully, to be vague and mystagogic. They tend to rely on some new power within us, some new experience which draws back the curtains of a dark, undefined mystery. This is the fate of those who would escape all charted regions. They are hypnotized by the night in which all cows are black. The odd result is that one can never tell whether the new heaven and the new experience are at the lowest or highest end of the scale of the values we are accustomed to recognize. It used to be said of an interpretation of Hegel that it left one in doubt whether his system was pure materialism or pure idealism, and that it could not matter as the two were only different sides of one another. The economic materialist has, as we know, made up his mind quite clearly what Hegel ought to have meant. Our great English thinker, Bradley, was also forced to describe the all-embracing experience which consummated life in terms of sensation, and Bergson, having given the cold shoulder to reason, is never able to free his readers from the uncertainty whether " intuition " means a swoon into ecstasy or into unconsciousness. And if the professional philosophers are at a loss, we need not wonder if the literary prophets of the day, like D. H. Lawrence and Middleton Murry, dash from one inconsistency to another.

This is true, and the blindness which their " seeing " has brought upon them might be used as an argument for the old orthodoxy and an illustration of the old belief that no one can presume to look on God and go unscathed. The fact, however, that at various times thinkers and prophets have arisen to tell us of some new and mystic way to happiness seems to imply that they must have had some, at any rate, apparent reason for their belief. And I do not think that we have far to seek for this reason. It is given to us by Brewster and it has been one of the recurrent complaints of man.

When we try to map out the spiritual heavens and penetrate into the secret of nature, we find ourselves baffled by the very weapons upon which we had at first merrily relied. We are like a boy who tries to reproduce all the rich coloured life of the countryside with the aid of a pencil or charcoal alone. Our thought seems to be limited by our own weakness, to be an expression of ourselves more than it is of the universe, and so it is that the imaginative artist despises dull reason, that Bergson dismisses it as a mere dummy in a shop window, and the mystic longs to be one with what is around him and above him and to throb in unison with its rhythms and pulsations. They would cast the slough of the reason and get rid of their discontent. Here Lawrence and Modernists of a certain variety join forces and make an odd company; the latter fall back on a religious experience which steeps them, as Thetis protected Achilles, against the assaults of science and its rationalists; and Lawrence longed for a " mystery, the reality of that which can never be known, vital, sensual reality that can never be transmuted into mind content, but remains outside, living body of darkness and silence and subtlety, the mystic body of reality."

Joined to this magic experience is a longing for invulnerability. The hero of *The Fountain* would at all costs reach this happy state and so live beyond good and evil as we divide them, beyond the familiar world of love and hate, excitement and disappointment. It is interesting to recall that some of the quietists in the seventeenth century taught that those who arrived at the stage of perfect quietude could no longer sin at all and that consequently they were free to do what they liked. This illusion, for such I must call it, is not as uncommon as might be expected, and it appears in the illuminism of several sects. It is noteworthy because it is so akin in spirit to the dream of invulnerability, the state of perfection in which one is so master of oneself that nothing can disturb the peace of the soul. Put this unperturbed state and the occult, esoteric experience together and we have the complete contrast with that of the Christian ideal. The language of both may have at times a similar sound, but the meanings intended diverge utterly.

Why then is this alternative so persuasive to many ? I have already suggested the answer in mentioning the discontent so many feel at the results achieved by our normal faculties. Is this discontent legitimate ? As the Christian saints have been conspicuous for a certain discontent, and as one of the greatest of them has enshrined this attitude in the ever-memorable words, " Thou hast made us for Thyself, and our hearts are uneasy until they shall rest in Thee," it might seem that we should have to answer in the affirmative. Yes, the answer is in the affirmative, but there is one mighty and decisive condition, and it is this condition which is not observed by all those of whom I have written. It is recorded in the principle already stated that God has accommodated His love and His atonement to man and

while so handicapping Himself and His power has nevertheless gained His end. It is we, let me repeat, who
disturbed the even motion of God's love at the beginning,
and it is we who by our desires expressed what we are in
the crucifixion of love. We thereby determined how
we must proceed if we would be perfect. " The
servant is not greater than his master," and if we humili-
ated God we must have been dishonest and dishonour-
able, the kind of people who are capable of tearing up
promises as scraps of paper, of bestowing the Judas kiss.
No wonder the precursor of Christ demanded a change
of heart, that the rough ways should be made smooth
and the crooked ways straight ! The decisive condition,
therefore, is that we should first recognize the truth
about ourselves, and that, in other words, is the recognition of the need, not as Brewster thought for an auto-da-
fé of ourselves, but for the virtue of humility.

To consider the ideal of life in the light of this principle
of humility is as sure a path to truth as it is to holiness
within one. Everything will be found to fit into place.
We have the reason why the human character, as we know
it in ourselves and in history, can be nicknamed Tantalus.
He is for ever tantalized by a vision of greatness which
he never achieves. There is in man a divorce between
what he should do and what he does, between the vision
and the reality, and even within the vision between the
glimpses of a land flowing with plenty and the arid
desert of his philosophy of it. He is like a deserted lover
who was never meant to live alone and beguiles himself

for a time with self-love. The story which Christianity
puts at the beginning is precisely a choice between the
divine love and this self-love, and it explains all that
happens subsequently by the doom of a foolish and
fatal choice. As man has so mistakenly exaggerated
his own worth and determined to rely on himself, God
takes man at his word and leaves him to discover by
bitter experience that it is not good to be alone and
that human dignity despoiled of the supernal love which
integrates and elevates it falls apart in an interior conflict,
in a scission of concupiscence and duty. The remedy
is again by humility. God who has taken man at his
word and delivered him to his desires now works to his
good through those desires. He becomes flesh and
blood, " humbles himself, taking the form of a servant,"
and still obedient to the will of man He is taken outside
a city and made into a figure of shame. But because
He has so identified Himself with man, His love and His
humility become man's propitiation and a new way is
opened to the highest of all ideals, union with God.
The tree of life was from henceforth to be the tree of
Golgotha, and the new message is given in the words
from a modern and intensely Christian poem :

> I tell you naught for your comfort,
> Yea, naught for your desire,
> Save that the sky grows darker yet
> And the sea rises higher.

Quick-seeing poets like Blake have told us that we can
hold infinite space in the palm of our hand. This glimpse

of a great truth has however seldom, outside Christianity, been recognized in its universal application. The Christian religion, having the example of its Master before it, assures man that he must begin with littleness if he is to reach infinity, and that the best illustration of littleness is himself. The modern substitutes all ignore that littleness and rely on something which never belonged to man at all ; they cry for the moon of ecstasy and complete happiness and they invent a mysterious power to get them what they want. That power is not theirs for the having for the reason that it does not exist. They would spring out of their skin by their own strength and with the same spring reach Nirvana. We all know that the name given to unholy dealings with supernatural forces is black magic, and though pseudo-mysticism does not deserve so bad a name as that, it is of the same family type. The Christian practice is so normal and history has proved it to be life-giving. We must begin with what we are, no matter whether the method prove dull or humiliating. It is, at any rate, common in the sense that it is not reserved for a clique, for " the heaviest hind may easily come silently and suddenly upon me in a lane." Nor need it be dull because our thoughts about the inmost wonder of the universe must be clothed in a language which appears inadequate. The Brewsters and the Middleton Murrys would throw away that thought ; the Christian takes it humbly as crumbs at least from the table, and as he tries to profit by what he is given he comes gradually to discover that thought and reason are not to be despised ; that there is a connection running up from what is our best to the ideal beyond all ideals ; the reason wherewith we have worked as with a talent put at our disposal turns out to be the coinage of God. It is marked with the superscription of truth and goodness, however faint the impression of the latter may be.

I can now sum up the argument of this chapter and its bearing on all that has so far been written. Its chief point can be expressed in the old Greek saying, " Know thyself." Those who have learned to know themselves, their weakness as well as their strength, will not be inclined to think that they can do easily without God or that what belongs to perfection can be had by their own unaided efforts. Their thoughts and expectations will be grounded in humility, and it is in conformity with this that the Christian religion demands of all an act of humility as the first step to the realization of its ideal. More significantly still, the Founder of Christianity, who is God as well as man, gives Himself the cosmic example of the way to life in being straitened as a man and suffering unto death on a cross. We have then the paradox that human nature as we know it can neither attain happiness without suffering nor perfection without the sacrifice of itself. Some of the reasons why this must be have been already given, and what now it is all important to see is that the drab and conventional parts of life must be willingly accepted and that the alternative ideals which have been examined all break down because they refuse to accept this cross. Their advocates, scandalized by such a gospel, cry out " Non serviam " and try to grasp substantially the dream which art sets before their eyes. And that this is not an unfair and unverified retort the experience of so many who have wandered in strange places proves. If poetry and music have been of inestimable benefit to man, the makers of them have seldom been happy, and they know full well that death takes them away even though the hope remain that " still are thy pleasant voices, thy nightingales awake."

Here again the evidence of Mr. Beaton's hero gives us the naked truth.

" This is happiness," I wished to say, looking at my cup off which the steam was curling and rising as from a lagoon in tropical forests. " This is beauty, life, truth, reality," looking at the sordid room and at the chattering women. " This, the appreciation of this, and the rejection of unreal daydreams is wisdom and philosophy."

And to show that this is a true change from the young and perhaps slightly superficial view that had once held him, the young man now is able to discern even in the spectacle of the miserable down-and-outs around him a beauty which is divine and preached by Christ.

For what else were they than the scapegoats of our society, the creatures destined to suffer all their lives in atonement for other's sins ? Their undeserved torments, their involuntary crimes would rise with the chanting of the nuns and the prayers of hermits to expiate—in that new assemblage of space and time where such adjustments are permitted—the gross inexcusable offences of the comfortable classes.

Here indeed we are much closer to reality than in all the fine words which have been uttered in praise of beauty as truth, of delectable moments when those who have been lucky in endowments and in material surroundings are free to forget the lot of the despoiled and the decrepit. " Day sings no song, neither is there room for rest beside night in her sleeping : life has left but a sigh for a song, and a deep sigh for a drum-beat." The searcher after truth must draw near to the mount of Purgatory before his eyes can see the mystery of life unveiled.

CHAPTER V

PER CRUCEM AD LUCEM

THE last part of our task now awaits us. Throughout the preceding chapters we have been engaged in making comparisons. The world is incurably idealistic in this sense, that it is for ever striving to provide itself with some ideal which will give it complete satisfaction. I have taken some representatives of this desire from modern writers who have not been content with the theistic and Christian ideal and tested their dreams by comparison of them with the majestic vision given to us in the thought of God and Christ. The conclusion was that they failed, but it was not denied that they may give us novelty and point to an experience which is free from the dull, circumscribed and pedestrian truth which Christianity seems to tolerate. But so far from this being a point in their favour I have argued that it is their condemnation and an additional proof of the truth of the Christian view of life. The pagan idealist always seeks either to bend our vision to this world exclusively and occupy himself and us with programmes of social reform or else he works upon some hope that he may find some retiring ground, some eyrie where, free from the dust of the arena, he may pass his days in a perpetual state of invulnerability and joy. The first of these can only momentarily delude a nation or a race. Men and women are not cured of all sorrow, of interior disappointment and the perverse will by legislation and classes and physical and social well-being. Othello may be a prince, but he is subject to jealousy and mad fits, and the longing of Psyche is not contented with mortal love. Nor, as we have seen, can the other alternative suffice; it may indeed be so untrue as to be dangerous for sanity. To indulge in beliefs about oneself which are not and cannot be verified is near to madness, and it makes little difference whether a man fancy himself to be an Apollo or an irresistible lover or a superman or endowed like a second Achilles with invulnerability. At best it is a romance or takes the form of an ambiguous and lonely mysticism, and it may be granted that it gives moments of joy and glimpses of a state of ineffable happiness. But this state is never achieved, and for the simple reason that it can scarcely be realized for any length of time in this life. This life is crowned with thorns, and full joy lies beyond our powers and belongs to another to give by grace and love.

The error which infects all these hopes and plans is the same. Their authors will not accept the conditions of human life, the shadows as well as the light. " By the river of life there is ever a wintry wind as well as

a heavenly sunshine." Few when they look at the
world of nature would be so foolish as to think that
its ends are attained without cost, but when they turn
to man they forget this and would have him perfect
without travail. The condition of man is indeed far
harder than that of other creatures ; he is not only by
nature forced to suffer and pass long laborious days
before he can attain manual and artistic skill and learning and satisfy his needs, but he is conscious of the
frustration and adds infinitely to his ennui and anguish
by his consciousness of it ; and moreover just where he
should be most secure he is weakest. His self-command
fails him unexpectedly and his motives can with such
infinite difficulty be kept high and single. He has an
enemy at court who is no other than himself. The
reluctance to acknowledge the good and the bad in
himself has been responsible for the many illusions of
perfection which he has entertained, and, as we have
seen, it is because he is untrue to himself that he rejected
Truth when it came, though that Truth had humbled
itself to accept the only conditions which man had
made possible, the only conditions too which allowed
for his restoration and union with divine good.

But if the Christian religion is to so many a stumbling
block and folly, it is to those who have the eyes to see
the power and the wisdom of God. Left without that
Revelation man can know something of God and why
he has been created. There is no excuse, therefore, for
seeking elsewhere than in God the happiness and per-

fection of the human race and the human individual. Nevertheless, the poverty of our knowledge should be a lesson to us and a motive for seeking for further light not from ourselves but from Him who is the source of beauty and truth ; and the haunting dream of bliss and invulnerability must be sought in Christianity and not in any natural religion or secret power-house of man. One last lesson, also, emerges. If our nature is such that we must labour to enjoy and if sin must be cauterized before health be restored, if, that is, the ultimate and consummate joy can come only by facing the worst, then we must be prepared to embrace the drab and the humdrum and all " the evil of the day." Those who profess Christianity or a love for Christ, if they think otherwise, have not learnt the meaning of His example. " He came unto his own and his own received him not." It is we who dictated the terms upon which the noblest of human lives should be led and we imposed the way of suffering which, as the disciple is not greater than his master, all true seekers of wisdom must follow.

The truth of this view of life is contained not only in the story of the suffering of the Son of God but also in the constantly repeated warnings that came from Him. These are usually formulated in terms of self-denial or suffering, the cross and death ; but in an age when death and savagery and evil have been as far as possible hidden away from the public gaze, when plagues and droughts, the crack of a pistol shot or flashing of a knife no longer disturb the minds of ordinary folk as they sit at home or hurry in tubes to business,[1] we may easily forget that the paradox of Christianity must be verified despite our favourite habits and clichés. " 'No,' said Miss Eliza, 'we cannot bind with phrases the boundless deity.' " "To withhold the truth from a human being is always wrong " : " We must get rid of all inhibitions " : " A healthy body means a healthy soul " : " The only genuine asceticism is in sincerity and the love of all things " : " Christ was, we know now, the great humanitarian."

These and many other assertions of the so-called modern spirit are in reality a denial of the saving truth of Christianity ; they are one and all an attempt to kick against the goad and they spring out of a fond desire to stifle the still small voice that whispers " fool." The silly soul within us is for ever longing to go on holiday, to rush off to the seaside and forget the office stool. But if it be a condition even of natural success

[1] Mr. Aldous Huxley has the same warning on the dangers of civilization in an article in *Everyman*.

" Civilized life is, for the most part, at once too safe and insufficiently natural. The moderately prosperous member of a civilized urban community inhabits a man-made universe, whose every detail has been designed by human beings for human beings. For years at a time he can live almost completely oblivious of the fact that there are such things as Nature and Chance, unaware of the alien malignities of the outer world and ignorant of the very meaning of such a word as ' risk.' But for many people a life that is too secure, too humanly convenient, tends to seem dull."

that a long apprenticeship is needed, if the fingers which glide over the keys and obey spontaneously the directing intelligence must first have submitted to long hours of drill, of scales and arpeggios, is it to be expected that instruction in the greatest of arts, the imitation of God and His Love, should come without effort or sacrifice ? It is so easy to talk of God in nature, " dreaming that of a sudden Thou shalt stand revealed in bud and bough." This spring-time of religious experience must pass, and the tests of love must come. When the bridegroom is by there is occasion of feasting, but when He is absent and hidden away in a strong guard-room, with spittle on His face and bruised and broken through our fault and thus winning the battle for our souls, it is monstrous that we should stand at the window complaining of His tardiness in coming and think only of enjoyment.

It is one of the difficulties of our human state that we cannot easily keep our gaze steadily on truth. We keep on tacking to the circumference ; every new and untasted pleasure draws us after it. At one moment what better than to live with a few friends ? then the talk and character of a new-comer diminishes that joy, and we think that there are better things to seek ; soon the brightness of this new ideal is clouded over and a more languorous excitement warms us. Or again the anxiety to be well known and well regarded, to be greeted with pleasure, to move in a circle which is quick to appreciate our witticisms and judgments, literary,

political and personal, these *idola fori* the chief motives
of our actions—for a while ; but soon the folly of living
by human respect, the narrowness of the horizon turn
us back on ourselves and we prefer to assume indifference or cultivate our garden or perhaps capture a peace
by striving to leave behind us an immortal poem or
discovery or work of scholarship. The various persons
we meet, the books we read continually add to the pattern
of our ideals and put their spells upon us. Partly
through contrasts and partly through novelty each new
experience tends to take all the colour out of the old ;
the undergraduate on holiday feels a distaste for the
life of learning and the crotchety and pedantic scholars ;
the rustic is seized with a feeling of envy and humilia-
tion as he walks in the crowded streets past the multitudinous shops of a city ; the stay-at-homes bewail
their moth-eaten souls when they listen to a modern
Walter Raleigh.

Thus we are subject to evanescent passions and aspirations and the glamour of what we have not tasted leads
us to make wrong contrasts. Yet the verdict of the
world is fairly constant, and just as we do not judge
the devotees of the intellectual life the most worthy
of all of our admiration—though surely our intellect
is our highest faculty—so we reck little of the life of
pure delight compared with that of sacrifice. The
reason is that our intellect feeds on the rind and lets
the juice escape and delight is meant to crown our
actions when the race is run. Christianity gives an

increasing meed of joy even to those who persevere
in the race and struggle, but it reserves the contemplation of Truth unveiled to an end yet to come.
This is not inhuman, for the world acts on the same
faith and is most willing to pay its tribute to those
who have endured pain and loss for a noble cause.
Not Epicurus but Christ is the figure it carries in its
heart.

As we look back on history and the lives of great
men and women it is not gay love, not even natural
mysticism which makes the deepest furrow in memory.
Certainly the debonair and the original are pleasing and
make a subject for a good story, but no more than the
plays of Bernard Shaw are they of much comfort to
us when others' lives and our own honour are at stake.
There is the story told of Clovis and his followers that
when they first heard of the Passion of Christ one of
them cried out, " Would that I had been there to slay
the rabble that dared crucify Him ! "   But another with
deeper insight into the Christian mystery corrected him
saying : " Nay rather, would that we had been there
to die with Him."   And there is little doubt but that
we love above all the picture of a Damien amongst
his lepers, a Peter Claver tending and nursing his black
slaves at Cartagena amid the stench of the filthy quarters
and suppurating sores, those who like the dying Jesuit
in Claudel's *Satin Slipper* are fastened as on a cross to
the stump of a mainmast and on that altar bring bless-
ings, " like that of Abel the shepherd," on the whole

world. Let us therefore by all means dream of a state
of bliss when there shall be nothing between us and
Supreme Beauty, nothing hiding nature and friends.
This, please God, will come in God's own time, but
we must not anticipate, not cherish illusions. We can
no more all be wise in the twinkling of an eye than we
can add a cubit to our stature, and it is not given to us
to enter into the joy of Christ till we have been made
fellow-sharers in His sufferings. *Que farai, fra Jacopone?*
Se' venuto al paragone. "Fra Jacopone, what wilt thou
do? Thou art come to the testing too." Da Todi
had learnt his lesson, that divine love is a fire which
burns and that the littlest of spiritual creatures must
go through a purgation before he is fit to mate with
God.

> All that I had to purchase Love I gave,
> Yea, all myself and the whole world in fee,
> And had Creation been all mine to have
> For Love would I have given it willingly.

Further proofs could be easily given of the supremacy
of the Christian doctrine. The nature of man as we
know it gives witness, and it is the only truth which
works. No parent, no statesman can afford to neglect
it. The child is destroyed by unalloyed pleasure, the
State by ease. Nor let it be said that the ideal which
is put forward as a rival to the Christian is unfairly
described in terms of pleasure. It is quite true that
we are given a vision by poets of communism, by lovers
of nature and by mystics of a scene where serenity

and mutual love may prevail; these dreams can be portrayed in words, but when they are translated into the concrete they mean a paradise where there is nothing to do, where the few can continue to exercise their rare gifts and the rest must be indulged. Already the far-seeing are troubled with the thought of a future when a perfected mechanism will have left mankind without a work to perform. They see that a world of unemployed, even though their condition be one of ease and security, will be far from a blessing, that virtue will be quickly sapped and tedium breed new troubles. The fact is that contentment is no lasting state with man unless he has achieved it after a life of superhuman effort. Even the effort must be of a singular kind. The honest work done by civil servants and in far fields does not usually bring in retirement the happiness which had been hoped. Only the saint can afford to be apparently idle, and the idleness is in reality a peace sustained by the highest intensity of will and the contemplation of an object of infinite love.

Now this natural law of change, of never abiding happily in one stay, which is symbolized for us in the rhythm of the seasons is obeyed also in the supernatural life vouchsafed by God to man. It might, perhaps, have been otherwise. Much may have depended on the choice the second jury of mankind passed when confronted with Incarnate Truth. It chose its own and our destiny: " for when he is come, he will convince the world of sin, and of justice and of judgement."

191

The best had to be through the worst, by the killing
in ourselves of what is best, by carrying a cross. No
doubt love makes all things easy, and the Love of
God transfigures all it touches, so that the law in our
members and in our perverted wills is overcome, and
what I have just said needs to be modified. But it is
at least necessary that we should understand our fate
and see that it is by the narrow way. To keep whispering to ourselves false consolations, to look for the end
when we are only at the beginning, to want, like Peer
Gynt, to go round instead of through pain, these are
but compromises with life and foster a lie within the
soul. When St. Paul spoke of the very earth travailing
to bring forth the meaning of God, he summed up the
function of nature and its service as a symbol of the
atoning love of Christ. On that higher plane all is
fulfilled in a mysterious way ; evil seems to triumph,
the Christian Church is ever in agony, saints are despised
or tortured and mystics undergo one long surprise of
pain vicariously for others. But the liturgy of Christen-
dom is, nevertheless, not the refrain of Job ; it does
not so much confess the mysterious ways of God as
enter into them ; initiated, its participant stretches out
his arms and they cover the sky like a great cross, for
In hoc signo vincit.

It remains to add a short word on how the Christian
ideal comes to be realized in the life of the individual.
The advent of it may come in an infinite variety of ways,
and those who would limit these ways to one, and even

allow a special time for it, are as children who expect
all happiness to be like birthday presents. Consistently
with this mistaken view some have desired to delay
baptism to adolescence; but this is not the command
of God nor the standard tradition of Christianity, and
the very fact that from the beginning the ideal of which
the people had fondly dreamed came true in the flowing
of water over an unwitting baby's head, marked the
terms of the new dispensation. Something which could
be adorned by sense but belonged to a far higher realm
of love and union, had been vouchsafed by man, something which even the most complete athlete in moral
and spiritual values would be unable to master. Hence
in a way it became immaterial how the divine life
germinated in the soul. To the babe it came uncon-
sciously, to many as something divinely obvious, to
others as a refreshment and cleansing, while to some it
might be in a still small voice or vivid experience.
The last way which is regarded often as the most
authentic is in truth the most open to illusion and disappointment. Carried away by the sense of victory,
of a new birth into invincible strength, it mistakes the
accompanying and passing experience for solid perfection which is far from being as yet attained. Just
as the lover in the first transports of passion endows
the fleeting moment with constancy, so too the convert
mistakes the rush of confidence for salvation. But
whatever be the mode of rebirth into the Christian ideal,
it has one chief characteristic and one promise for the

future. This characteristic is the firm guarantee or assurance of a definite way and a settled end. *Incipe, parve puer, risu cognoscere matrem.* Not so much with a smile, perhaps, as with a contentment of mind despite the necessity at times of giving up almost all one cared for in this world. There is a recognition ; uncertainty disappears and something corresponding to visible sight is given to the mind in its discernment of the plan of the invisible world. The duty of assenting to God who is realized within as Lord of the conscience and its destiny and without as a felicitous providence stretching from end to end of nature known and unknown, this duty stirs the will to action to make His will our way and our peace. In our everyday choices we choose between this and that, rejoicing at times that we have been matched with this hour or soberly following the dictates of a sure conscience. But we do not so much choose some means in assenting to the Christian faith as accept the universe, accept ourselves and all that we imply. We start again with God first, with God as more to us than our own life or the life of the whole world. We do not choose ; we are chosen ; we are lifted up out of that darkness in which we have lived knowing only the tangible and the present certainty, moving by guess work and with arms outstretched to hold what is near. The invisible world becomes more real than the visible, giving it form as the meaning of a word changes the character of a few visible scratches before our eyes. And it belongs to the essence of this

new choice to have something final in it, to be a yea
or nay to the question of our own worth and the significance of everything connected with us, an exit from
the womb, a moving into the world of eternity where
a supreme Judge and Lover " heeds but hides, bodes
but abides."

The character of this new life has already been
described in general terms. It is a movement like to
the seasons and the days and nights; there is winter
as well as summer, night as well as day; but in contrast to the cycle of the years and the days there is growth
in the soul, a garnering and an increase which never
withers and dies not even at the touch of physical death.
The secret of success on the way is that " we be mindful
of our condition." " For which of you having a mind
to build a tower, does not first sit down and count the
cost, whether he hath the wherewithal to finish it:
Or what king, about to go to war against another king,
will not first sit down and take counsel whether he be
able, with ten thousand, to meet him that with twenty
thousand comes against him ? . . . So likewise every
one of you that does not renounce all that he possesses
cannot be my disciple." The conditions of our life
lie first in the human nature which is ours with its
dignity and its infirmity and secondly in the altitude
of the end to which we are called. The past is strewn
with bright suggestions for happiness, all of which
failed because they promised success in the twinkling
of an eye or by some simple recipe. Even in the

domains of art what attractive formulas have been produced time and again, and the young take them up, write and talk vehemently and irreverently of the stupid theories of their parents and older friends, and after a time are cured themselves by experience. Few can be serenely confident and at the same time ready to count the cost. Those who take up some religious belief so often expect immediate returns and even console themselves with an imaginary dividend to justify their life to their friends. But the parable which I have quoted does not end on a note of relief. Instead it has the stark command to renounce all possessions.

Those therefore who have embraced Christianity do not ask for a new thrill, neither do they expect a state of " invulnerability " or halcyon peace or even a special providence which will prevent them from being molested. On the contrary, they arm themselves for the worst, and if too much pleasure comes they begin to suspect that they have been " offered all the kingdoms of this world " and must have made a compromise. They are not carpet knights ; they are not even clothed in their own strength, but in that of " one who comforts them." The time for feasting with the bridegroom has ended, for the bridegroom has been slain and cries in the words of the medieval plaint,

> "Look unto mine hands,
> These gloves were given me when I her sought ;
> They be not white but red and wan,
> Embroidered with blood my spouse them brought.

See Love hath shod me wonder strait,
Buckled my feet with sharpe nails,
Quia Amore Langueo."

It is strange that many who call themselves followers
of Christ are so unwilling to walk after the manner of
His life and take His yoke upon them.   They are scandalized by suffering and invent alternative theories of
Christianity to that which their Founder taught again
and again.   They seem to be rationalizing and not
reasoning, to be converting what is a natural fear of
the hard into a denial of its place in the Christian dispensation ; and the result is that they see nettles everywhere and hate the rose because of the thorn.   God in
His goodness tempers the wind to the shorn lamb, and
there is no oppression in the Christian religion.   As I
have already said, this religion is one of triumph, of
man standing on the towers of dawn, but the craven
in us will not listen and wishes to be tucked away from
" the beasties that go bump in the night."   Of course,
there are an infinite number of differences between one
man and another man in courage, sensitiveness and
pertinacity, just as there are some who seem always to
live sheltered days while others are buffeted by every
evil fortune.   That in certain moods, exhausted and
broken we should stretch out our hands in longing
for a further shore or a new vision on this side of
the river is forgivable.   What is not so forgivable is
that we should cozen ourselves into a belief that this
vision is really at hand and throw down our arms.

197

Those beautiful lines, set to music in Brahm's Requiem, " Lord, make me to know what the measure of my days may be, let me know all my frailty, ere death overtake me," should be written in the soul of every man. Until we realize our frailty, the frailty of our nature and our individual character, and realize it calmly and without suppressions, there is no advance to any existing ideal. Humility is not the easiest of virtues, and there are those who would identify it with a slavish outlook, a quality unworthy of a noble religion. But it is stronger than any nordic or pagan pride. The humble can join hands and sacrifice their position and self-esteem for a cause, whereas the proud are friendless and tyrannical. No co-operation, in fact, is possible unless this despised virtue be present, save under the stress of a passing excitement or concealed ambition. There is a passage in Ruskin's *Crown of Wild Olive* which is so much to the point and so likely to be forgotten that I must quote it.

Men who know their place can take it and keep it, be it low or high, contentedly and firmly ; neither yielding nor grasping ; and the harmony of hand and thought follows, rendering all great deeds of Art possible—deeds in which the souls of men meet like the window-jewels of Aladdin's palace, the little gems and the large all equally pure, needing no cement but the fitting of facets ; while the associative work of immodest men is all jointless and astir with worldly ambition ; putridly dissolute and for ever on the crawl ; so that if it come together for a time, it can only be by metamorphism through flash of volcanic fire out of the vale of Siddim, vitrifying the clay of it and fastening the slime, only to end in wilder scattering, according to the fate of those oldest, mightiest, immodestest of builders, of whom it is told in scorn, " They had brick for stone and slime had they for mortar."

Of the experiences which follow on the assent of faith and the gesture of humility it is better to be silent. They have certain well-defined features, but for the rest they differ with each individual, for God knows each one of His own by name. It must always be remembered that the Christian story involves two, and that to relate the private and separate history of a Christian is to leave out the most important part, that is, the secret drawing of the soul by God into Himself. It is secret and it is paradoxically an experience for a time of intense loneliness as the self sloughs its skin and suffers a transformation during which the old things are for a time of no meaning and of no avail. Most of our joys have at least the tang of sense clinging to them. Thought has to draw near to a fire and warm the hands in front of it before it becomes active and inspired, and loves die in absence. But in the intimacy of the soul with God there is at first no feeling of presence, no voice to be heard, no hand to be felt, no face to be seen. It is as if one were talking to oneself, and were it not for some ineradicable, intellectual certainty which persists against all the appearances, we should be tempted to abandon this religious life as make-believe. A jogtrot along a high-fenced road instead of all that romance we had dreamed of; and if daringly we take our life in our hands and throw ourselves out of our ken to find our heart's desire, we meet " cliffs of fall, frightful, sheer, no-man fathomed."

And yet it is just because we are promised no easy

journeying that something deep down within us begins
to sing as a musical instrument responds to the right
note, and as " all things," in Aristotle's great phrase,
" sing together with truth." We cannot free ourselves
from the conviction that nobility needs testing, that
greatness is acquired by suffering and that love spells
sacrifice, and even were this not so the symbol of the
Son of God crucified has taught mankind its best wisdom
and the only means whereby human loves and human
ideals can be exalted beyond the stars.

This is far from the humanism and the dream of
ever-increasing joy which is preached in novels and
essays to-day. That many should seek " to build a
better world," " a country fit for heroes to live in,"
does them credit, and it is natural, perhaps, that some
of these should be dazzled by the prospect of Elysian
fields shining out in contrast with the dark inferno of
industrial cities with their foul air and begrimed streets.
But such passionate sympathy should not lead to a falsi-
fication of the law of life and virtue. Because there is
unfair sorrow and distress we must not think that justice
deals out happiness as Rhadamanthus dealt out doom.
Death and ill-health and accident and grief cannot be
banished by any human formula, and the weaknesses
attendant on human nature, sloth and self-indulgence,
envy and hatred, can be eradicated only by each man
taking up his cross and conquering himself. By contrast with the dull and agonizing present all else looks
pleasant, but the pleasant fades when it is touched and

there is no enduring joy save one. Paradoxically he that gives his life shall find it, and death and life meet only in mutual support when it is a God who increases in us when we decrease. Gradually as the divine love takes shape in us the old bitterness departs, the old human valuations give place to something more affectionate, more understanding and more generous. The petty ambitions which fill the papers, which drive men and women to such follies and vices, to supplanting their neighbours, to boasting and lying, look like the lines of a face seen under a microscope. There is no sense of superiority or priggishness, no judgment of degree of fault. " There but for the grace of God go I." We need so much a change in our scale of values ; the suffering poor are tempted by what they have not, like starving children before the window of a confectioner ; the rich who get little pleasure out of their riches, but know that luxury has made them incapable of enjoying simpler pleasures, protest against all change in the name of some dummy ideal ; the plebeian apes his betters and the " betters " have given up all thought of an after-life and make plans for society without a soul. " What doth it profit . . . ? " Like Lazarus risen from the tomb the Christian cannot but feel that everything is topsy-turvy, that people are more interested in cards and dicing than Love dying on a cross. His first instinct is to release Love and to flay the crowd for its indifference, but it is part of his new insight into truth, that he will instead choose to die with Christ.

He has learnt that love and sacrifice cannot be separated as long as sin is committed and enjoyed.

The truth contained in the expression, to grasp the nettle, holds also for the religious life, and Mr. Buchman puts his finger on the essential of religion when he demands as the initial act for members of the Group Movement a complete self-surrender to God. Where, as it seems, the Group Movement is mistaken is in taking an act as a habit and assuming that the whole of an organic growth is possessed already in the embryo in the womb. To begin whole-heartedly, without any reservations or conditions, means that the end is already half achieved. No movement in history has succeeded, save by the most lucky accident and for a very brief time, without the undivided enthusiasm of its leaders and followers. We know quite well how in cases of mental indecision, of scruples, bad habits and moral failures, the advice always tendered by experts is that the new choice must be absolute and final. The force of one motive and ideal, be it wrong or right, is like a dam released, a dog or wolf amongst sheep. Minorities govern according to the strength of their passion and their belief; they stop at nothing and are not troubled with doubts which delay the will. Islam has conquered by one idea and Russia to-day has wisely from its own point of view drawn a cordon round its people's belief and thereby insured for one generation at least a drastic effect for its own propaganda.

But for one principle or idea to bear the test of time and be an ultimate good to its believers it must be capable of expansion and be fit to embrace and harmonize the myriad experiences and truths which man must encounter in his passage through time. It is vain for Mr. Buchman to salute the consecrated will as perfect. Love has many windows and has need of learning and wisdom, and the life of the Christian calls for the exercise of every faculty and all that is in him. His life is hid with Christ. By interior renunciation he is for ever freeing himself that the divine love may penetrate all his actions, that his judgment of events and policies and of his neighbour may be not only well-intentioned but wise. He has to be in the world and not of it, to mingle rights with duties, to combine the interests of individuals with groups, groups with nations and nations with the civilized world; he must adjust the claims of beauty and morals, liberty with control and authority, learning with tradition and faith. It is the claim of the Christian faith that it neglects none of these things. All the partial and momentary salvations preached sound shrill and foolish compared with the plenitude of the Christian faith. It is Christianity alone which knows what is in man, has regard for his dignity when an age decries it, bids him be modest when a liberalistic, evolutionary doctrine would pet and pander to his liberty, demands of him thought and a disciplined mind, throws beauty in his way and exalts a married love above the vicissitudes of time. But above all it is Christianity alone which faces pain and toil, and seeing that love is sacrifice puts before man the symbol of the Son of God crucified as the one sure way which leads to life, and that eternal.

Date Due			